Pathways

A Primer for Family Literacy Program Design and Development

by Rebecca King
and Jennifer McMaster

**National Center
for Family Literacy**

© 2000 by National Center for Family Literacy

ISBN: 1-884458-06-8

Acknowledgements

The National Center for Family Literacy would like to thank all of the programs we've worked with through the years, who have taught us the fundamentals of program design by example and who have broadened our understanding of the very practical realities faced each day by family literacy programs. The indefatigable courage and unflinching ingenuity displayed by programs nationwide give meaning to our work and hope to all families. Specifically, we would like to thank those programs that let us include brief case histories of their work-focused program adaptations: the Family Literacy Program in Long Beach, California (Judith Carey, Program Coordinator, and Roberta Lanterman, Family Literacy Director); the Canton City Schools Even Start program in Canton, Ohio (Jane Meyer, Program Coordinator); and the Careers for Families initiative in Louisville, Kentucky (LaDonna Roser, Program Coordinator.)

The authors would like to thank readers Nicole McLean (NCFL), Beverly Gatlin Bing (consultant with Kentucky Even Start) and Mary Gwen Wheeler (NCFL), all of whom offered tremendous insight throughout the drafting process. We would also like to thank the entire Training, Program, Policy, Research, External Relations and Operations departments of NCFL who provided many answers, resources and wisdom.

Finally, we gratefully acknowledge the overwhelming commitment to improving the education and well-being of families that has been exhibited by the William R. Kenan, Jr. Charitable Trust, the Toyota Motor Corporation, the Bureau of Indian Affairs, the John S. and James L. Knight Foundation, and The UPS Foundation. It is only with their support of family literacy initiatives, and the support of partners like them, that NCFL has been able to study and promote the family literacy approach that you will read about in this book.

Dear Family Literacy Champion,

I'm gladly greeting you as a family literacy champion because I know already that you want the best for families, and that you believe that the best includes education for adults and children alike. That subtle philosophy—parents and children learning together—sets you, and family literacy, apart from many other educational approaches.

It's with great excitement that I introduce this guide to you—more than ten years in the making, the best practices accumulated by the staff at NCFL, based on the experiences of thousands of practitioners all across the country who have made family literacy their calling. And I challenge you to not only read the words, but read between the lines. Ask yourself, always, how can I make this work for the families in my community? This book can't answer that question. Only you can.

Family literacy has grown quickly from a handful of local programs to a national movement. That movement has mirrored the journey that so many families have taken as they embrace literacy as a means to expand their life experiences and discover their potential. Hopefully this guide will help you discover your potential as a family literacy champion.

Let me also say that there is a real urgency for services for families. While we want to share the successes with you, we also want you to remember that there are many families who slip through the cracks, who need more comprehensive services, who are battling so many complex issues that it's sometimes difficult to know where to start. This, I say to you, is your charge. Every family is worth your effort.

NCFL has been so fortunate to have collaborated with dedicated practitioners, business partners, service agencies, researchers and politicians through the years. We've also had the chance to meet many families—the true heroes of family literacy. It's from the families that we glean our most important lesson—that all families have strengths, and that powerful programs are built on those powerful family strengths.

It is with this in mind that we distill our knowledge into what we hope will be a very practical guide to starting and sustaining a quality family literacy program. We are convinced that good planning and implementing sound practices from the inception of a family literacy program will produce programs that can truly address the needs of families and build strong communities of learners.

On a more personal note, I want to acknowledge the two authors of this book for their outstanding commitment and expansive expertise. Jennifer McMaster has helped set to words the complexities of family literacy in a straightforward way that everyone can rally around. And I particularly want to recognize Becky King, who is the guiding light of NCFL family literacy program development. For ten years, Becky has helped shape the family literacy movement, within NCFL, and on a national level with her involvement in Even Start and many other local and state family literacy initiatives. If you are half as excited as I am that we've been able to get an ounce of Becky's knowledge and know-how into print, then you will most definitely benefit from her insights. And family literacy will be the better for it.

You're starting on an incredible journey. Dig in, and enjoy.

Sharon Darling

Sharon Darling
President and Founder
National Center for Family Literacy

Table of Contents

Preface:
A Historical Overview
of Family Literacy

Sometimes, to figure out where we are, it's helpful to know where we've come from. What follows is a very brief history of the the national family literacy movement and the National Center for Family Literacy's involvement in that movement. You may find this information useful in talking with others about family literacy, or you may just find the information interesting. Or, you may be so excited about getting started right away in developing a family literacy program that you jump ahead to Chapter 1 (but be sure to come back and read about the history later—you might be surprised and energized by the way family literacy has evolved.)

Early Steps: Educational Reform, PACE, Even Start and the Founding of NCFL

The development of family literacy as an approach to level the educational playing field for impoverished adults and children is rooted in the national educational shift that began in the 1980s. As a concerned nation began focusing on student achievement, legislators and educators stressed the importance of community, policy and parental support in order to reach higher academic standards.

By 1988, under the leadership of U.S. Representative William Goodling, the Even Start Family Literacy program was authorized as part of Chapter 1 (now Title I) of the Improving America's Schools Act. In 1989, President George Bush and the nation's governors developed the National Education Goals. Two of the original six goals (there would be eight when signed into law in 1994) addressed literacy directly and family literacy indirectly. Goal One, titled "School Readiness," intended that, among other things, "every parent in the United States will be a child's first teacher and devote time each day to helping such parent's preschool child learn, and parents will have access to the training and support parents need." Goal Six, titled "Adult Literacy and Lifelong Learning," looked to a future when "every adult American will be literate and will possess the knowledge and skills necessary to compete in a global economy and exercise the rights and responsibilities of citizenship." This goal also states as one of its objectives that schools will implement comprehensive parent involvement programs.

Three years prior to these federal efforts, Kentucky had successfully implemented an innovative literacy program that garnered national attention: the Parent and Child Education (PACE) program.

PACE: The 70% Solution

In 1985, there were areas in Kentucky where 70% of the adults did not have a high school diploma, and 70% of their children dropped out of school before completion.[1] To address the educational needs of Kentucky's most impoverished families, Kentucky Assemblyman and Chairman of the House Education Committee Roger Noe, Early Childhood Education specialist Jeanne Heberle, and Sharon Darling, who at that time served as Kentucky's Director of Adult Education, developed a new educational program that would soon change the direction of literacy programs in all 50 states.

[1] Brizius, Jack A. and Susan A. Foster, *Generation to Generation*, High/Scope Press, 1993, pg. 28.

PACE was designed to meet the educational needs of parents and their children together. The program schooled parents and caregivers in language, math and social studies in preparation for the GED while offering parenting courses and structured parent-child interaction time.

By the end of 1985, PACE legislation was enacted, making Kentucky the first state in the country to pass a family literacy law. Six pilot sites were selected for program implementation and study in rural counties. In 1987, the scope of PACE expanded to include 18 rural counties, and at its height PACE reached into some 36 counties. Soon, PACE and Kentucky could claim a new statistic: 70% of the adults enrolled in PACE obtained their GED or raised their reading test scores by at least two grade levels.[2]

Just three years after its inception, PACE was selected in 1988 by the Ford Foundation and Harvard University's Kennedy School of Government as one of 10 outstanding innovations in state and local government, and was awarded $100,000. Today, state-funded family literacy programs in Kentucky continue to flourish.

The Kenan Model

As the PACE program was setting an example for educational reform in Kentucky and throughout the nation, it captured the attention of one organization that was looking for ways to improve education specifically in North Carolina. In 1988 the William R. Kenan, Jr. Charitable Trust of Chapel Hill provided a major grant to develop programs in three inner-city sites in Louisville and four communities in North Carolina: Marshall, Henderson, Fayetteville and Wilmington. The Kenan Trust was further interested in developing model family literacy programs that could be duplicated in any setting in the country. The PACE

[2] *Ibid*

model was modified to broaden parental eligibility, include more parent-child interaction time, require parents to volunteer at schools, and provide more teacher training and career education.

More than 300 families participated in the first two years (1988-89) of the Kenan program. Early findings indicated that both adults and their children made important gains as a result of attending family literacy programs. A follow-up study in 1991 found that one year after leaving the program, 66% of adults were either in some form of higher or continuing education program, had definite plans for enrolling or were employed.[3] The study also showed that after two years, none of the children had been held back in school, and over 75% of the children were rated by their current kindergarten or grade-school teachers as average or above average in both academic and social areas.

Establishing the National Center for Family Literacy

The success of the Kenan Model attracted even more attention and a barrage of requests for information—more than 5,000 from around the country. It seemed clear that there was a need for a centralized office charged with the responsibility of dissemination and training in the emerging field of family literacy. In July 1989, a grant from the Kenan Trust established the National Center for Family Literacy (NCFL), and provided funds to support the first year of operations, with Sharon Darling at the helm. By August of 1989, NCFL had begun a major training and technical assistance program.

Throughout the 1990s, NCFL guided the practice of family literacy through improvements in teaching approaches, research, advocacy, and program development and adaptation to meet the demands of legislative, economic and social change. Today, NCFL continues to

---

[3] *Follow-up Study of the Impact of the Kenan Trust Model for Family Literacy*, NCFL, 1991.

create programs and support them through advocacy, research and dissemination. NCFL's training department has delivered training and technical assistance to family literacy staff and others in all 50 states and three foreign countries. As part of NCFL's advocacy efforts, staff frequently deliver keynote speeches year-round to national and local groups, and provide testimony to Congressional committees.

Private Funders Support Public Cause

The history of the development of family literacy throughout the United States would look quite different were it not for the almost immediate and urgent support of several large and committed corporate partners. Among them, the Toyota Motor Corporation has helped NCFL launch, train and evaluate numerous programs for families with preschool-aged children beginning in 1991, and, more recently, elementary school-aged children. From the start, Toyota's innovative approach to funding set the tone for the collaborative growth of family literacy, showing that private funds can support public funds and create collaboration around a national initiative.

Other private funders, such as the John S. and James L. Knight Foundation and The UPS Foundation, have focused dollars and expertise on using the family literacy approach to help move low-income families to economic stability. From development programs supported by these and many other private funders, an extensive body of intrinsic information about effective program implementation has been gathered and disseminated widely to practitioners and administrators in the family literacy field, as well as to educational researchers, legislators and the public.

The National Family Literacy Movement

Even as the PACE program was put into place in Kentucky, elsewhere throughout the nation thoughts had already turned to literacy and building on a family foundation. In 1987, Washington state developed and passed family literacy legislation, Project Even Start, preceding the federal program of the same name by a year. As word about family literacy spread, many governors and state legislators began examining the possibilities family literacy offered.

In 1988, Representative Goodling sponsored the legislation that created Even Start through the Hawkins-Stafford Elementary and Secondary Education Improvement Act. In 1991, the National Literacy Act officially renamed Even Start to include family literacy as part of its title—now the Even Start Family Literacy Program—and also made community-based and nonprofit organizations eligible for funding. In the 1991 Fiscal Year, nearly 240 Even Start grants were awarded. At that time, Even Start administration was shifted to the state level, because appropriations had passed the predetermined $50 million mark.

In the 1998 program year, Even Start served more than 39,500 families in 732 projects. In just ten years, Even Start programs have expanded their reach by more than 37,000 families. NCFL has provided training to approximately 50% of the Even Start staff nationally.

In 1989, as the Education Summit produced the National Education Goals, First Lady Barbara Bush helped establish the Barbara Bush Foundation for Family Literacy, a private nonprofit organization that aids communities in starting family literacy programs as well as raises public awareness of family literacy nationwide. The National Education Goals were later signed into law by President Bill Clinton as the Goals 2000: Educate America Act, on March 31, 1994. By that time, there were eight educational goals, including the "Parental Participation" goal. This goal proposes that "every school will promote partnerships that will increase parental involvement and participation in promoting the social, emotional, and academic growth of children," making it the third goal out of eight to reflect the growing value placed on family literacy.

In 1991, Head Start, which falls under the auspices of the U.S. Department of Health and Human Services, announced the Head Start Family Literacy Initiative, and in 1992 an amendment to Head Start addressed parental involvement requirements. The 1994 Head Start

Act included a federal definition of family literacy and legislated family literacy as one of seven priority areas for newly funded state collaboration projects. Since its inception in 1965, Head Start has served low-income children and their families, and national leaders began early to promote active involvement of local Head Start providers in family literacy efforts. The Head Start Family Literacy Initiative emphasizes literacy skills development for parents, so that they can become more effective as their child's first teacher. In 1998, Head Start was reauthorized and this reauthorization included an expanded definition of family literacy consistent with other federal laws, promoting intensive, comprehensive models of family literacy.

The National Literacy Act of 1991 also established the National Institute for Literacy (NIFL), which serves as a focal point for public and private activities that support the development of high-quality regional, state and national literacy services. NIFL's goal is to ensure that all Americans with literacy needs have access to services that can help them gain the basic skills necessary for success in the workplace, family and community in the 21st century. Some of NIFL's primary activities include promoting adult literacy system reform through Equipped for the Future (EFF), a long-term consensus-building initiative that developed content standards to ensure that every adult can gain the knowledge and skills needed to fulfill real-world responsibilities as workers, parents and citizens; bringing technology to the literacy field through LINCS, a state-of-the-art Internet-based information retrieval and communication system; improving services to adults with learning disabilities; and providing Congress, the literacy field and the general public with timely information about policy matters relating to literacy.

Title I (previously Chapter 1)—Helping Disadvantaged Children Meet High Standards—of the Elementary and Secondary Education Act of 1965 was expanded in 1989 to include Even Start and was reauthorized in 1994 to include further support for family literacy in school reform efforts. As of the writing of this guide, reauthorization of Title I is underway.

In 1996, Congress passed the Personal Responsibility and Work Opportunity Reconciliation Act (PRWORA), commonly referred to as welfare reform. This law has had a profozund impact on many of the families that family literacy targets. PRWORA abolished the individual federal entitlement to Aid to Families with Dependent Children (AFDC), as well as the JOBS and Emergency Assistance programs. These three programs were replaced with the Temporary Assistance for Needy Families (TANF) block grant to states. All states were required to implement TANF by July 1, 1997. In contrast to the open-ended funding commitment of AFDC, now federal funding to states is capped at historic levels. Further, new time limits and work requirements were imposed on welfare recipients, marking a dramatic shift to a "work first" philosophy throughout the nation. In family literacy programs, PRWORA has necessitated program adaptation in areas such as curriculum, program design and community/business partnerships.

The Workforce Investment Act (WIA) of 1998 was passed into law in August, 1998, and includes, as Title II, the Adult Education and Family Literacy Act. This Act contains provisions in the law that specify family literacy as a viable option to meet adult education and literacy needs. One of the purposes of this act is to "assist adults who are parents to obtain the educational skills necessary to become full partners in the educational development of their children." Through the "one-stop" career centers and workforce investment boards mandated by WIA, adult education and family literacy providers are encouraged to partner with job training and placement agencies.

The 105th Congress (1997-98), which passed the Adult Education and Family Literacy Act, passed three major pieces of legislation that affected five laws by, among other things, including a consistent federal definition of family literacy services throughout the legislation.

"The term 'family literacy services' means services that are of sufficient intensity in terms of hours, and of sufficient duration, to make sustainable changes in a family and that integrate all of the following activities:

(A)   Interactive literacy activities between parents and their children.

(B)   Training for parents regarding how to be the primary teacher for their children and full partners in the education of their children.

(C) Parent literacy training that leads to economic self-sufficiency.

(D) An age-appropriate education to prepare children for success in school and life experiences."

Legislation that contains this definition includes the Workforce Investment Act, the Reading Excellence Act, Even Start, Head Start, and the Community Services Block Grant Act. This definition is supported by a federal emphasis on collaboration at the state and local levels, allowing for easier blending of funding, more opportunities for staff development, and greater resources for the delivery of services to families.

As you begin or continue your journey in family literacy, seek out new ways to draw from this rich history of challenges and successes. Over the years, a strong national foundation for family literacy has been built so that communities like yours have better, more comprehensive resources on which to build. Every community and state has unique strengths and needs—now, more than ever, it's time to make the most of the opportunities available.

Chapter 1:
Why Family Literacy?

The family is one of the most powerful indicators of success for future generations. The economic stability of parents can and will affect the paths open to their children and the choices children will make along the journey. For some families, education may take a back seat to priorities such as financial well-being, health, and safety—not by choice, but by necessity or lack of opportunity. Yet research has shown that education can lead to economic and physical security, as well as to less easily defined outcomes such as confidence, self-value, and empowerment.

One in three American children will be poor at some point in their childhood.[4] It's important to remember, though, that children aren't poor—their parents are. There are any number of factors that contribute to poverty. But one factor remains consistent in study after study: low educational attainment.

[4] *The State of America's Children Yearbook*, Children's Defense Fund, 2000

The intergenerational cycle of poverty and limited education is a difficult one to break. The pressures on families are enormous, and the barriers to self-sufficiency often seem insurmountable. For parents who have repeatedly met with failure, a sense of hope can be even harder to obtain than a job, a house or a car. For children, growing up in poverty can paint a bleak picture for the future.

Family literacy can work to break the cycle of undereducation; it can help families create a legacy for future success because family literacy works with the whole family—parents and children learning together. It builds on families' abilities, and draws from the power of the family. Family literacy works *for* the family. And subsequently, it works for the community, the nation, the economy, and society at large.

Family literacy builds on and supports "family" strengths as well as "literacy" strengths. It reinforces the parents' status as their children's first and most important teacher. It utilizes the latest brain research that values interaction and nurturing in early childhood to support healthy mental development. It recognizes that a child's academic success is related to the child's early educational experiences, and it offers children a foundation for learning that they carry with them through elementary school and beyond. It works with parents and primary caregivers to create a learning environment in the home. It shows parents how they can make a difference in their lives—and the lives of their families—by increasing their basic skills and language acquisition. It helps adults break out of the isolation sometimes caused by poverty, and points them toward new avenues of opportunities in their communities. Family literacy teaches families that they can learn together, that learning is a mutual process, that learning is fun, and that learning has a beneficial emotional and social impact as well as a financial one.

What is Literacy?

Through the years, the definition of literacy has expanded to address the essential skills needed for children and especially adults to succeed in a number of roles. No longer is it acceptable for a functioning member of society in America merely to read and write. While reading and writing are certainly important foundations, there are many other necessary skills that families need in order to achieve economic independence and establish a stable home environment. Clearly, literacy means more than the ability to read and write, especially for those adults and children for whom educational inequities are only one barrier to overcome.

The National Literacy Act of 1991 defined literacy as the following:

> "Literacy is an individual's ability to read, write, and speak in English, and compute and solve problems at levels of proficiency necessary to function on the job and in society, to achieve one's goals and develop one's knowledge and potential."

Interestingly, the Workforce Investment Act of 1998 defines literacy in almost the same words, but note the slight difference:

> "The term 'literacy' means an individual's ability to read, write, and speak in English, compute, and solve problems, at levels of proficiency necessary to function on the job, *in the family of the individual,* and in society." (italics added)

Literacy, at least legislatively, has come to reflect the needs of the adult learner as worker, family member and citizen, which are roles identified by the National Institute for Literacy's Equipped for the Future project. This federal definition is also beginning to address, at least peripherally, the many populations in the United States for whom English is their second language.

Goal One of the National Educational Goals states that "all children in America will start school ready to learn." The objectives of this goal focus on access to preparatory programs, nutrition and healthcare for children, and the value of parental involvement early on as a child's first teacher. The objectives also address parents' needs for training and support in their family capacity.

In this case, legislation chooses to define a child's school readiness partially by the interaction the child has with his or her parent. It also reflects the knowledge that parental involvement in a child's early learning experiences will likely have positive effects on the child's future academic achievement.

Legislative definitions of the term "literacy," as the term applies to either adult or child, have evolved to keep up with the changing social, economic and political climates of the country, the workplace, and the individual. It will be important that the public's perceptions of "literacy" also continue to expand, to increase the understanding of what it means to be "literate" and what it takes to achieve the skills necessary to succeed.

Defining the Family

Families define themselves. While there are legal definitions of "family" that serve various purposes, the concept of family has by necessity grown to include any number of structures.

In the case of family literacy, a family is comprised of a child or children and the adult or adults who are primarily responsible for a child's well-being and who are consistently an influence on a child's development. This is intentionally a vague description. For the families that family literacy intends to serve, boundaries of the traditional family structure are often expanded to include siblings and extended family members, custodial grandparents, neighbors and friends, or legal guardians.

Family can encompass aunts, uncles, foster parents, grandparents, legal guardians, brothers and sisters, neighbors or other members of the community, grandchildren, nieces, nephews, cousins, and foster children; they can be of one ethnicity or several; they can live together in one housing structure, or sometimes they can live separate from one another, yet maintain a constant relationship. What is important in working with families is to recognize and respect their diversity, and never try to mold them into a preconception of what a "family" should be.

Defining Family Literacy

All families have some level of family literacy, if we interpret family literacy to mean the passing of knowledge from one generation to the next—indeed, to that end, family literacy is hard to avoid.

Keeping in mind the expanded scope of the federal definition of literacy in the Worforce Investment Act, consider again the federal definition of family literacy:

> "The term 'family literacy services' means services that are of sufficient intensity in terms of hours, and of sufficient duration, to make sustainable changes in a family, and that integrate all of the following activities:
>
> (A) Interactive literacy activities between parents and their children.
>
> (B) Training for parents regarding how to be the primary teacher for their children and full partners in the education of their children.
>
> (C) Parent literacy training that leads to economic self-sufficiency.
>
> (D) An age-appropriate education to prepare children for success in school and life experiences."

This definition is a great place to start. But it certainly doesn't describe how a quality family literacy program operates or achieves its goals in meeting the needs of families.

NCFL's approach to family literacy is a holistic, fully integrated family-focused design that targets parents and children most in need of improving their literacy skills, which often translates to families living at the lowest economic levels. These families may live in urban or rural communities; they often represent a variety of cultures; many receive public aid or have in the recent past; and they all have significant educational and non-educational barriers that stand in the way of obtaining meaningful employment, academic success, and economic stability.

For the purposes of this guide, we use the term "family literacy" as an abbreviation for "comprehensive, integrated family literacy services or programs." By comprehensive we mean the complete inclusion of four components—adult education, children's education, Parent Time, and Parent and Child Together Time. By integrated, we mean a program design that deliberately coordinates learning activities across all four components.

The four components of family literacy described below reflect those outlined in federal legislation, and are the core components that will be used for discussion throughout this guide.

Adult Education

Adult education in comprehensive family literacy programs begins with the foundations for learning—basic skills and English language skills. But it also offers more than that. In addition to building adult learners' educational and employable skills, the adult education component recognizes the importance of helping adults learn what are sometimes referred to as "soft skills," such as critical and creative thinking, problem solving and interpersonal skills. Emphasis is placed on the goals that parents set for themselves, both academically and personally. Within a family literacy program, the skills parents learn in adult education can be applied to their home life as well as on the job.

Children's Education

In the early history of family literacy programs, the children's education component focused on the developmental skills of preschool children, emphasizing emergent literacy skills, to better prepare children for academic and social success when they began school.

Now, the focus is expanding to include curriculum and program design that addresses the needs of school-age students. Some family literacy programs also provide services to enhance the development of infants and toddlers. Because family literacy works with children in the context of their families, programs also recognize that children are affected by a parent's transition from welfare to work, and studies are looking at ways that this can be addressed in the curriculum. The difference between family literacy programs and child-focused programs is that family literacy works with children in relation to their families. By attending to the goals of both parents and children, family literacy programs: 1) increase interaction between children and parents, 2) facilitate active learning for both children and parents, 3) increase parents' support of children's learning, and 4) transfer learning activities into the home.

Parent Time

Parents or other primary caregivers who enroll in family literacy programs bring with them various strengths as well as a myriad of difficult obstacles to overcome. Parent Time in a family literacy program is an opportunity for adults to share their concerns and their strategies for dealing with home issues and day-to-day challenges. The primary focus of Parent Time is on improving parenting skills, particularly by strengthening parents' understanding and support of their children's literacy development and early school success. By also working on other life skills in Parent Time, parents can increase areas such as self-esteem and confidence to help them provide a more stable home environment for their children. One useful approach in Parent Time is to draw on local resources, inviting community speakers to work with parents on a range of issues that may include health services and care, mental health services, tax or legal advice, housing issues, substance abuse or domestic violence. Parent Time also works to improve interpersonal skills, communication, and offers parents the chance to both give and receive peer support.

Parent and Child Together (PACT) Time

PACT Time is more than setting aside "quality time" for children and parents to play together. In an early childhood setting, it is a regularly scheduled session during which parents, focusing on their children's interests and with support from staff, learn how to support their children's learning through play. In an elementary school setting, the parent-child interaction may revolve around an assigned school task or particular school event, again with an emphasis on developing an educational relationship between parents and children. The reciprocal learning that takes place during this time offers parents and children a chance to become true partners in education. This time also allows parents to practice effective parenting behaviors and methods in an environment conducive to learning, with professional instruction available if and when questions arise. Parents and staff will debrief the PACT Time experience, to further discuss children's literacy and behavioral development. One of the goals of PACT Time is to help parents learn how to transfer literacy activities to the home, to foster a learning relationship between parents and children outside the classroom setting. Family literacy practitioners have noticed an added benefit of PACT Time in addressing some of the "gaps" many adult learners have in their own early education experiences. By playing with their children and learning more about supporting each phase of their children's learning, parents often discover or rediscover missing keys to their own understanding of basic concepts. PACT Time is unique to family literacy, and sets it apart from other literacy programs.

Component Integration

The integration of the four components of family literacy within the curriculum and throughout the planning and implementation of a family literacy program is crucial to the building of a quality program, and even more crucial to the success of the families enrolled. Research by NCFL has found consistent evidence of the gains made by both children and adults in comprehensive family literacy programs:

- Adults participating in family literacy programs demonstrate greater gains in literacy than adults in adult-focused programs. Adult family literacy students typically increase their basic academic skills by 1.5 grade levels during the program year.

- Participants in family literacy programs are more likely to remain in the program than participants in stand-alone programs. Seventy-three percent of families complete the program year, enroll in another educational or training program, or get a job.

- Children participating in family literacy programs demonstrate greater gains than children in child-focused programs do. While in family literacy programs, children make gains in language and literacy, as well as other important areas such as creativity, social relations and initiative, that are three times greater than expected as a result of normal maturation.[5]

It cannot be said enough times—the whole is greater than the sum of its parts. Component integration is key to the success of family literacy. The significance of each individual component is heightened by the impact of a well-integrated program. This requires cross-training and teamwork among the instructional staff in planning curriculum and program design. The most effective use of the four components is a methodical, cohesive approach. In quality family literacy programs, the enrolled adult is viewed as a part of a family, and the enrolled child as part of a family. That family will become stronger when treated as a whole, rather than a collection of stand-alone parts.

As family literacy programs adapt to the particular circumstances and needs of the families enrolled, the configuration of programs must also be flexible. Some programs that focus on families with preschool children are able to meet at a school or community center in a schedule that resembles a school day, with parents and children attending classes at the same time. A combination of center-based and home-based services provides flexibility as well as the added effectiveness of learning in both environments. Programs that work with elementary school-aged children must accommodate the school system's schedule and available facilities, while other programs with a large population of working parents must

[5] *Facts & Figures* (unpublished, NCFL) and *The Power of Family Literacy*, NCFL, 1996

adapt to fit job schedules. These variations can make the integration of components challenging, especially the coordination of PACT Time. However, with a little extra effort and creativity, component integration can—and will—pay off in the end.

Goals of a Quality Family Literacy Program

Specific goals, and there will be many, of individual family literacy programs will vary depending on the needs of the population that a particular program serves. Below are listed some very basic goals to consider as you begin to formulate an action plan for implementing a family literacy program:

- Enhance the educational level of parents; improve basic skills, life skills and English language skills.

- Help parents develop skills and knowledge needed to become employed or to pursue further education or training.

- Provide training for parents to support their child's literacy development and participate as full partners in the education of their children; encourage parents to become familiar with, and comfortable in, school settings.

- Increase the developmental skills of preschool children to better prepare them for future success in school; increase the academic achievement of school-aged children.

- Address the literacy and social skill needs of school-aged children to improve school performance.

- Improve parenting skills among adult participants and introduce parenting strategies.

- Enhance the relationship between parent and child through planned, regular time together.

Challenges Facing Adult Learners

Family literacy programs are designed for those most in need of services. Therefore, most adults in family literacy programs come from the following populations:

Teen Parents—About once a minute an American adolescent has a baby; every year about one million adolescents become pregnant. Compared with older women, most adolescent mothers are neither financially nor emotionally prepared for parenthood. They face higher risks of postponed education and welfare dependency. (*Starting Points: Meeting the Needs of Our Youngest Children*, Carnegie Corporation of New York, 1994.)

Single Mothers—Women increasingly face the demands of child rearing alone. By 1989 almost one-fourth of all children lived with only one parent; women head 90% of single-parent families. (*Starting Points: Meeting the Needs of Our Youngest Children*, Carnegie Corporation of New York, 1994.)

Undereducated Parents—Almost half of mothers dependent on welfare do not have a high school diploma. (US Census Bureau, 1995.) Eighty-four percent of unemployed fathers and 82% of unemployed mothers lack a high school diploma. (*The State of Literacy in America*, National Institute for Literacy, 1998.)

Those with Learning Disabilities—Thirty-five percent of students identified with learning disabilities drop out of high school. This is twice the rate of their non-disabled peers (this does not include the students who are not identified and drop out.) Sixty percent of adults with severe literacy problems have undetected or untreated learning disabilities. ("National Adult Literacy and Learning Disabilities," 1994, in *Learning Disabilities, Report of the Summit on Learning Disabilities*, National Center for Learning Disabilities, 1994.)

Immigrant Populations—The number of ESL students in family literacy programs is growing rapidly. All programs should share the goal of enhancing the literacy development of immigrant, non-English-speaking parents and their children. Program designs vary depending on the participants' needs, the language and age groups served, the geographic location of the project, and the type of educational or community-based organization administering the project. (Gail Weinstein and Elizabeth Quintero, Eds., *Immigrant Learners and Their Families*, Delta Systems, Inc., 1995.)

Children and Poverty

Children from disadvantaged backgrounds often begin school behind their more advantaged peers; this lack of school readiness has seriously damaging effects on their self-esteem and greatly reduces their chances for later academic success. Too often the next steps are dropping out of school, early pregnancy, unemployment or underemployment.

One in five American children (19.9%) lives in poverty. (*The State of America's Children Yearbook*, Children's Defense Fund, 1999.)

During 1995, fewer than half of all three- to five-year-olds with family incomes of $40,000 or less were enrolled in preschool, compared to 82% of children from families with incomes of more than $75,000 per year. (*Years of Promise*, Carnegie Corporation of New York, 1996.)

As many as one-third of American students entering the K-12 system need extra help to keep up with their peers... Fewer than one-half of eligible low-income three- and four-year-olds receive Head Start services. (*Years of Promise*, Carnegie Corporation of New York, 1996.)

As homelessness continues to grow both domestically and internationally, there will be an even greater effect on large numbers of children. Only by intervening while families are still experiencing homelessness and as they make the transition to a stable, housed lifestyle, can the damage to literacy development be ameliorated. (*Journal of Children and Poverty*, Institute for Children and Poverty, 1996.)

The number of working poor families has hit a record high. In 1997, 3.7 million families with children lived in poverty despite being headed by someone who worked all or part of the year—the highest number in the 23 years for which these figures exist. (*The State of America's Children Yearbook*, Children's Defense Fund, 1999.)

"Children from low income families may have been read aloud to as little as 25 hours total prior to entering first grade while children from middle income families typically have been read to 1250 hours." (Dr. William Teale, Professor of Education at University of Illinois, Chicago.)

Families and Education

Despite the limitations of poverty and undereducation, parents are powerful:

Three decades of research have shown that parental participation improves student learning. This is true whether the child is in preschool or the upper grades, whether the family is rich or poor, whether the parents finished high school. (*Strong Families, Strong Schools*, U.S. Department of Education, 1994.)

Children's literacy levels are strongly linked to the educational levels of their parents—especially their mothers. A mother's education has more effect than other variables, including socio-economic level. (*The Literacy Beat*, Newsletter of the Education Writers Association, June 1988, vol. 2. no. 4.)

Higher maternal education is associated with higher levels of cognitive and emotional support for child development. (*Five Million Children: Our Nation's Poorest Citizens*, National Center for Children in Poverty, 1992.)

Children are short-changed when adults are overlooked. Better-educated parents produce better-educated children. Better-educated adults demand and get better schooling for their children. Better-educated parents produce safer communities conducive to learning. Better-educated adults are more productive for society. (Tom Sticht, *Report on Literacy Programs*, October 27, 1994.)

Early education has a positive effect on the family. Across all projects studied in a consortium of studies of the long-term effects of preschool intervention programs, Lazer, et al (1982) reported significant effects on students' school competence, attitudes about self and school and effects upon families. Mothers of preschool program graduates were more satisfied with their children's school performance and had higher occupational aspirations for their children than mothers whose children had no preschool experience. Children's participation in a high-quality active learning preschool program created the framework for adult success. (*High/Scope Perry Preschool Study*, High/Scope Educational Research Foundation, 1993.)

Households headed by better-educated adults are more likely to have books, computers, and an atmosphere where academic success is valued. (*The State of Literacy in America*, National Institute for Literacy, 1998.)

Quality Family Literacy Programs

Adult Education Component

Attention to non-educational and educational needs

Joint parent/teacher initiated approach

Balance of group and individual instruction

Interdisciplinary curriculum

Cooperative learning strategies

Critical and creative thinking mode

Pre-vocational training

Ongoing appropriate assessment

Appropriate reading instruction

Children's Education Component

Attention to non-educational and educational needs

Specific and developmentally appropriate curriculum

Authentic, developmentally appropriate assessment

Appropriate teacher/child ratio

Small group size

Parental involvement

Partnership between parents and teachers in planning and implementing curriculum

Literacy development

- ✓ Build upon strengths
- ✓ Empower families
- ✓ Incorporate assessment into instruction
- ✓ Facilitate active learning
- ✓ Integrate components
- ✓ Include some home-based services
- ✓ Celebrate diversity
- ✓ Collaborate with community service providers
- ✓ Use a team-planning approach
- ✓ Secure qualified staff
- ✓ Provide systematic and ongoing staff development
- ✓ Document outcomes in all components
- ✓ Make referrals to work, job training, work preparation

Parent Time Component

Opportunity to learn about child literacy development and cognitive processes

Parenting skills

Content driven by self-identified interests and needs of parents

Information for family growth and employment

Mutual peer support

Advocacy and referral services/ single point of referral

Coping and problem solving strategies

Opportunity for group activities/projects

Parent and Child Together (PACT) Time Component

Intergenerational component

Child-centered activity

Opportunity for positive parent/ child interaction

Opportunity to practice newly acquired skills

Staff in supportive role

Activities to support transfer to home

Opportunity for parents to develop observation skills

Chapter 2:
Assessing the Need for Family Literacy in Your Community

Chances are you have already assessed that your community could benefit (or currently does benefit) from a comprehensive family literacy program—otherwise, you might not be reading this guide! However, a formal community assessment is vital to laying a solid foundation for a new family literacy program. And, like many of the steps listed in subsequent chapters, community assessment is an ongoing process that can and should be used in maintaining an existing family literacy program to ensure that it continues to be relevant and effective in meeting the changing needs of your community.

A community assessment serves three purposes:

1. It generates documentation of the need for a quality family literacy program in your community. This documentation can then be used to seek funding and other non-financial support for the program from local, state and national sources (public and private.)

2. It assesses the interest level of other agencies, organizations and businesses in your community, enabling you to begin pursuing and establishing the many collaborative

partnerships which are essential to providing quality, comprehensive family literacy services.

3. It helps you to begin identifying your target population. Your program design will have to reflect this population in its curriculum as well as in practical concerns of program design such as site location and transportation. Information about your target population can also help you design recruitment strategies around the interests of potential students.

Assessing the community includes:

- Defining the community
- Defining the target population
- Organizing and analyzing data
- Determining how family literacy will "fit" in the community
- Examining how welfare reform impacts the community

Initial Data Collection

In order to work with and in your community, you must first establish what and where that community is. This may be determined geographically, as in city or county boundaries or by school districts. In more rural areas, the community may need to be determined by the location of families and their access to a centralized facility, or by the access that your program will have to those families. Your community may be defined through a particular place of employment with a high rate of working parents, or some other circumstance that calls out for a family literacy program. It may also be determined that several sites will be needed to serve all the families in your community. In many cases, however, the "community" will be defined by the service boundaries of the organization establishing the family literacy program.

Before developing your own community assessment, gather community assessments already completed by agencies such as local schools, community foundations, Title I, Head Start, the Chamber of Commerce, United Way, family resource centers, and others interested in serving disadvantaged families. As you review these assessments, look for gaps in services that family literacy could address.

The next step is to define your target population. Who are they in terms of descriptors? Where do they live? There are many resources from which you may draw demographic information. These can include resources obtainable through the school districts such as enrollment forms completed by parents, surveys the school has conducted through newsletters or other mailings, and documentation regarding the number of students receiving free or reduced lunches at the school. Census information and assessments done through city or county governments can provide a variety of information about the economic and social makeup of the community. Assessments done by other organizations, like advocacy groups that serve similar populations, may already have the answers to some of the questions you'll be asking.

There are several other substantial resources you may wish to examine. *The State of Literacy in America* provides estimates of adult literacy proficiency at local, state and national levels, prepared by Stephen Reder of Portland State University for the U.S. Department of Education, Office of Adult and Vocational Education (available on-line through the CASAS Web site at http://www.casas.org or by calling the National Institute for Literacy at 1-800-228-8813). Another to consider is the Annie E. Casey Foundation's Kids Count, which provides detailed information about children and families for a single state and the entire nation. This database is available on-line at www.aecf.org, or you may call (410) 547-6600.

You may also want to research other family or related program initiatives, like Head Start or state-supported adult education or early childhood programs, that are required to conduct assessments on a regular basis. Other resources for demographic information can include state employment agencies, the chamber of commerce, a board of realtors, local workforce investment boards, and state or local cabinets for human resources. Your local librarian may be able to help you locate demographic information available at the public library.

Sifting through data to determine the target population may seem tedious as you search for relevant statistics and make comparisons to national trends. In making the case for your family literacy program you'll need accurate, up-to-date information to support your proposal. Although this data collection can seem cumbersome, remember that numbers can be a powerful way to communicate the need for family literacy programs to outsiders and insiders as well, and it's helpful to be prepared with a variety of useful information, some of which may have more meaning for one group of potential collaborators or another.

To establish a base for comparison, identify the total population in the area or environment that you have defined as your community. Now, answer the following questions and consider how those answers reflect and impact your community. Bear in mind that most, but possibly not all, of the questions below will pertain to your program. You may wish to break down some of your answers further into census tracts.

- How many adults in your community did not complete high school? How many adults did not complete 9th grade? How many adults are in the lowest level of the National Adult Literacy Survey? In the bottom two (out of five) levels?

- What percentage of the adults needing adult education services is being reached at present?

- How many children receive free or reduced-price lunches at the public schools? What percentage of the total school population receives free or reduced-price lunches?

- What percentage of preschool-age children in the community is enrolled in pre-school or day care? What percentage is not being served?

- How many people in your community live beneath the national poverty level? How many of them are children under the age of five? How many of them are elementary school-aged children? How many households living at or below the poverty level are headed by single parents?

- What is the average age of the parents or caregivers in your community? How many teen parents live in your community?

- What is the unemployment rate in your community? How does this compare to the national level? (Be careful, as some studies of unemployment include only those adults who are looking for work. Often those parents who lack literacy skills have lost hope and are not actively seeking employment.) Are there geographical pockets of poverty in your community?

- What are the labor needs in the community? Do employers report a "skills gap" for entry level workers?

- What is the average income rate for families? How does this compare to the national level? What is the cost of living in your community—high, medium, low?

- How many households are receiving public assistance? How many have received public assistance within the past year? Within the past two years?

- What are the housing costs in your community? What are the rental costs, and what percentage do they represent of average family incomes? Is public housing available at reduced costs?

- What is the ethnic breakdown of your community? How many adults in your community consider English to be a second language?

- What gaps in services for disadvantaged families can you identify? What needs are not being met by existing agencies and organizations?

Once you've charted the results from your demographic poll, the nature and extent of your target population will be well on its way to being defined. It may be helpful at this point to construct a sentence that describes your target population that you can use as you begin interviewing other service organizations in your community, such as: "In specific areas of our community there is a high concentration of families living below the poverty level—families in which the parents have not completed their high school education and in which the children are beginning or are in school."

Further Analysis

Based on this initial data collection, there are some very broad questions to analyze, which will help you determine the potential scope of family literacy in your community. What are the educational and non-educational needs of the families in your community, particularly the families at the lowest ends of the economic spectrum? For example, do the adults in your community want or need to obtain their GED, learn English or complete vocational training? Are they facing new mandates as a result of welfare reform—are they required to become employed within a certain time frame and therefore must concentrate on improving their marketable skills? Are violence, poor housing or a lack of healthcare affecting the lives of the children in the families? Where do these families live? Where are existing services located and what population do they serve? What services or sequence of services can programs offer that will motivate parents and their children to enroll in a family literacy program?

As you consider these questions they may well lead you to ask other questions that are more specific to the needs in your community and the goals of your target population. In these beginning stages, try to keep an open mind. Try not to restrict the potential of family literacy's impact or your community's potential to support a family literacy program. Also, don't limit the possibilities of the families you hope to reach—their strengths will guide the direction of a family literacy program. When you begin to structure your program design, you will be able to distill your action plan into a manageable size with attainable goals.

Other Services Available — Great "Think-Abouts"

The next step is to determine if and how a family literacy program will fit with the other services available in your community. Head Start and other agencies may have a directory of community services. Avoiding duplication of existing services is necessary in effective planning. The best resources for this sort of assessment are the other organizations and agencies themselves. Find out all you can through their published materials, including brochures, newsletters, annual reports and Web pages before asking for a phone conference or a meeting.

When collecting information about the community, you can also take this opportunity to document other organizations' opinions on the need for family literacy services, as well as to survey their interest in working collaboratively with a family literacy program. Be sure to keep records of their comments and get their permission, when possible and appropriate, to use their comments as testimonials for grant-writing or public awareness purposes.

Before contacting other agencies, you should have a ready and thorough understanding of family literacy and the potential configurations a program might adapt (center-based, home-based, after school or work activities, etc.) to meet the needs of the target population. This information will help you clearly describe the program's potential, and will make it easier to communicate how a family literacy program could augment or support existing services. Interviewing key personnel in other support services can provide you with many valuable details about operating a program in your community; these interviews may be conducted either by phone or person-to-person.

Sample Phone Survey

Background Information and Introduction

Hello, this is _____. I am with *(your organization)*_____.
We are exploring community needs and current services offered. Your agency was suggested to us as one that we should contact. Who in your agency would be the best person to discuss your connections to programs that serve families (adults and children)? Is this a convenient time to talk?

(Briefly share information about your organization and your interest in family literacy.)

We need to learn what is currently available to families and if there is a need and an interest in creating family literacy programs in *(your community)*_____.

Survey

Agency:

Contact name and position:

Agency Information:

What services or programs are offered by your agency that connect to family literacy (adult- or child-related, or both)?

Describe the program(s):

Goals or intent of service/program:

Partners (other agencies/organizations):

Target population and requirements for participation:

How to enroll (recruit):

Is there a waiting list?

Have you done a community needs assessment or other survey that provides information about families, adults, children, etc.? Can you share the information?

General Community Information:

What other programs are you familiar with in the community that serve the same population?

Who else should we talk with to get a good overview of family education efforts in the community?

Do you think there is a need for family literacy programs in the community?

Do you know of any barriers to building new family literacy programs in the community?

May we have your permission to use your comments in the materials we develop to support family literacy in the community?

The following are suggested topics for investigation in your community. Again, remember that not all these subjects may be applicable to your community, and that there may be other types of organizations or services that you think it would be beneficial to pursue in your particular circumstance.

- Are there free or reduced-cost health services, social services, crisis services, housing assistance or legal assistance available? For adults or children or both? What agencies provide these services and how many families do they serve? What are the eligibility criteria for those families?

- Is there public transportation in your community? If so, what are its hours of operation, the areas it serves and the cost? Is there a reduced cost available? Is there another transportation option (e.g., school bus donation)?

- Is there a Head Start or other early childhood program operating locally? What other agencies collaborate with Head Start in your community to provide educational and non-educational services to parents?

- Are there any adult or community education services available? What fees do they charge, if any? What specifically do these services provide (e.g., adult basic education, GED preparation, job training, parenting skills)?

- Are there services available for preschool children, and are these services educational or non-educational? Are there after-school programs operating for at-risk children and/or their parents?

- What parent involvement activities are sponsored by the local school system?

- Are there women's centers in your community, and if so, what educational and non-educational services do they provide? Are there any organizations that specifically work with fathers and male partners?

- Are there cultural centers for adults or families who speak languages other than English, and do they offer educational or job-training programs?

- Is there a library association, local college and/or high school program that offers tutoring for children or adults? If so, what population do they primarily serve?

- Are there advocacy organizations or campaigns that support literacy or educational programs? Are there agencies that implement welfare reform strategies, job preparation and training?

- Is there a local office of the United Way in your community? This organization may be a centralized database and/or contact for a variety of services provided to families in need.

How are other service agencies and organizations funded? You don't need to know specific sources (unless they offer the information!) but it may be helpful to know if most community agencies are funded by public or private sources from the national, state or local level. It may also be useful to be aware of general fund-raising practices in your community, and how accustomed other agencies are to funding programs collaboratively.

Community Assessment and Welfare Reform

The population that most family literacy programs intend to serve is directly affected by welfare reform and the "work first" philosophy that many states are adopting. Consequently, your community and many of the agencies with which you'll want to build collaborations are likely to be affected by current welfare reform requirements and strategies.

As you analyze and develop your community assessment for use in applying to potential funding sources, become as familiar as possible with the ways that state and local welfare requirements affect your community and the families who will enroll in the program. Below are some questions to take into consideration as you are completing your community assessment.

What are the specific laws for your state regarding receipt of public assistance and use of welfare funds? What are the time restrictions that apply to your community and the families in your community? What activities are considered as meeting work requirements? Does your state have a family cap that determines when aid can be denied to additional children born to families on welfare? Are different groups of people eligible for different types and levels of assistance depending on the number and age of children, literacy levels, the age of the parent (e.g., teen parents) or other barriers to employment?

What are the immediate and long-term effects of current public assistance policy on your community? How many adults in your target population are affected by welfare mandates, immediately and in the foreseeable future? How many families? (You may wish to contact your local newspaper to see if they have reported on the current or recent impact of welfare reform in your community.)

Conduct at least an informal economic scan to find out the overall status of employment in your area. Which, if any, industries are hiring? Are they hiring for trained, entry-level positions? Are they capable of or willing to train at the workplace? Do they have any child care programs in place for working parents? What are starting salaries? What other benefits do employers' offer for workers and their families?

Talk to potential employers in your area. What skills do they find lacking in applicants? What skills do they specifically look for in new hires? What educational levels do they require? Are these employers willing to hire welfare-to-work employees, i.e., those with little or no practical job experience? Are they interested in working with or accommodating post-employment family literacy programs, either in or outside the workplace? It can be difficult or intimidating to contact employers "cold"—especially when you're requesting information about their hiring practices. Some family literacy programs have found it helpful to enlist the aid and support of a business or industry leader in order to gain entry to other potential employers.

What has become clear in the early years of welfare reform is that creative, flexible approaches to the design and delivery of family literacy services are crucial in terms of both curriculum and program structure. Collaborations with potential employers are an essential strategy to help former recipients make the transition from welfare to work, and the earlier you begin working with employers the more knowledgeable they'll be of what family literacy and its students have to offer. Also, it has become evident that the most effective relationship between welfare offices and family literacy programs is a reciprocal one. You will want to involve your local welfare agency in the earliest steps of planning your family literacy program, and help them understand how family literacy can work for their clients.

Other Community Assessment Considerations

Families who live below the poverty level, with parents who have not completed their high school education and who have children, and families who have recently received or are currently receiving public assistance are prime candidates for family literacy programs. Family literacy programs are designed for those most in need of services. Most adults in family literacy programs come from the following populations: families on welfare or who recently received assistance, teen parents, single mothers, parents who did not complete their high school education, those with learning disabilities, and populations for whom English is a second language. Many family literacy programs also have worked effectively with American Indian families, homeless families, prison populations and migrant workers. Your community assessment and the target population it helps define most likely will represent more than one of these categories.

If your estimated target population for recruitment is approximately 75 families or more, there are probably enough families to warrant a family literacy program (remembering that not all families will enroll.) Generally, you may expect to serve 10-20 families at a program site at any given time, but don't let this number inhibit or exclude any of your recruitment efforts and don't be surprised if this number fluctuates from year to year as the economy and the legislation change. Further, the number of families you work with will depend on the configuration of your program, that is, the shape of your program model and the services you provide. For example, you may not have 20 families who attend classes every day for six hours a day, but you may work with 15 additional families through home visits, or you may have adult learners who are in vocational training in another location or who are meeting work requirements by volunteering in their children's schools.

Beginning with your community assessment, starting a family literacy program may take six months to a year lead-in time—be patient, as there are many, many elements to bring into play. The initial planning stages are so crucial to developing a quality family literacy program, it's extremely important to allow enough time to put all the necessary pieces in place. Remember, it could be a year (or even longer, under some circumstances) before a program can offer truly comprehensive family literacy services.

It's worth repeating: Do not try to do this alone! Assessments are a great way to plant the seeds for future collaborations. Initial interest in starting a family literacy program in your community may come from parents, educators, librarians, business people, community leaders, or other service organizations. The most successful family literacy programs work in conjunction with school systems and administrators, social agencies, community organizations, welfare offices and public officials. Asking for their advice and support during this initial planning will lay the groundwork for the collaborations that will support and strengthen the program. It also will help you avoid duplication of services or inter-agency "competition" for participants. Especially if other organizations or agencies who are working with similar populations are unfamiliar with family literacy, you may experience some resistance at first. It may appear to them that you are "muscling in on their territory." Be sensitive to these perceptions—and reinforce the idea that you are not taking away from any existing programs. You are trying to establish mutual support systems so that you can integrate services at the local level, making those services more efficient and more comprehensive.

Be sure also to involve public officials as early as possible in these early stages—their advocacy can help give your program a solid foundation in your community. Use the community assessment to gauge officials' opinions on family literacy, with collaborative relationships as the ultimate goal. As you begin to establish partnerships with other members and agencies in your community, keep in mind that it is critical that everyone in your collaborative group—which will include people from institutions and organizations outside your program—have the same vision of your program's target population. A family literacy program cannot be all things to all people, and the focus should always remain on those families most in need.

Community assessments do focus on data and numbers, but the information they provide goes deeper than just raw statistics. When you take those statistics and apply them to the real lives of the families and the difference you believe your family literacy program can make, well-documented assessments become a valuable tool in support of the need for comprehensive family literacy services in your community. Use the information from your community assessment as a catalyst to gain support for family literacy, remembering that beyond the numbers are disadvantaged parents and children.

Chapter 3:
Creating Collaborative Partnerships

Although you're usually a team player, and despite the numerous warnings that will appear throughout this guide, you are convinced that the best way to start and maintain a family literacy program is to do it all yourself—or through the resources of a single agency. This chapter is intended to convince you otherwise!

If it were even possible to orchestrate a fully functioning family literacy program alone, there are still many other reasons to form partnerships besides helping to spread the responsibility of this enormous undertaking. Collaborating with other agencies and organizations makes programs stronger by increasing the efficiency of the delivery of services, as well as filling gaps in those services. Collaborating services can help consolidate available resources for families, and pooling resources will make it more likely that families will receive all the services they need. Working in partnerships can be extremely rewarding, not only in terms of blending funding but in gaining additional insight, expertise and a vast array of resources that reach far beyond money.

Most importantly, collaboration makes a program more effective for families in part because it makes the receipt of services easier for families, who likely are struggling with more than one issue at a time and who have needs and goals outside the educational realm. Rather than having to approach multiple agencies to meet multiple needs, families can enroll in comprehensive family literacy programs that offer services and referrals to services from a coordinated vantage point. Because the very nature of family literacy programs is that they work with both parents and children in educational and non-educational areas, family literacy is especially well suited to address the multitude of issues faced by adults, children, and subsequently, families as a whole.

Collaboration makes a program more effective for families in part because it makes the receipt of services easier for families.

Collaborative partners aren't necessarily funders, although we certainly hope that some of them are! There are many resources a family literacy program needs other than financial support (although financial support is crucial, too!). It is important, also, to think of your funders as collaborative partners who will help you make decisions about program design and implementation.

The most common core collaboration in family literacy is between an adult education provider and a children's education (either elementary or early childhood) provider. Other typical configurations of collaborations include volunteer literacy organizations, family support services and community-based organizations.

Circles of Collaboration

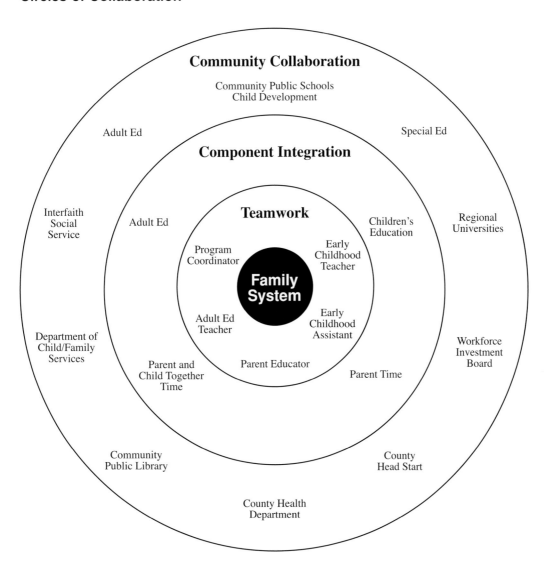

Community Collaboration

Community Public Schools
Child Development

Adult Ed

Special Ed

Component Integration

Interfaith
Social
Service

Adult Ed

Teamwork

Children's
Education

Regional
Universities

Program
Coordinator

Early
Childhood
Teacher

**Family
System**

Department of
Child/Family
Services

Adult Ed
Teacher

Early
Childhood
Assistant

Workforce
Investment
Board

Parent and
Child Together
Time

Parent Educator

Parent Time

Community
Public Library

County
Head Start

County Health
Department

For financial support, there are many ways a business, foundation, agency or organization can help, all of which have a monetary value. There are grants, in-kind donations such as supplies and equipment, donations of services, and volunteerism. Remember that financial supporters will not write you a blank check, and that funds will have to be carefully accounted for. Also, some, if not most, supporters will want something in addition to the knowledge that they are supporting a worthy program, whether it's a mention in your annual report, a logo on your National Family Literacy Day® banner, or a quarterly progress report that shows via your evaluation system that your program is achieving its goals and making improvements. To put it simply—honor all your partners! Share credit, successes, challenges and triumphs. More specific funding considerations will be discussed later in this chapter.

Collaborative partners also include other agencies who will work with you to deliver necessary services to enrolled families. They may also include civic organizations who help you raise community awareness, local employers who are willing to advise you in developing a job skills curriculum, literacy organizations who provide tutor training, and many others (see the Potential Partners section which follows).

In all of your collaborative partnerships, you will want to create a "win-win" relationship—for example, offering reciprocal referrals, blending funding streams for overall fiscal stability, coordinating marketing efforts, providing evaluation assistance, or making use of facilities to their fullest extent. Find out what "counts" for the other organizations with which you wish to partner—number of families served, hours of service, number of GEDs received, job placement—and then make sure you count those things. Always remember, though, that your goal in building collaborations is to ensure that families have the best resources available to them. This, too, should matter to your partners.

Potential Partners

In their *Collaboration Handbook: Creating, Sustaining and Enjoying the Journey*, Michael Winer and Karen Ray define collaboration this way:

"Collaboration is a mutually beneficial and well-defined relationship entered into by two or more organizations to achieve results they are more likely to achieve together than alone."[6]

As you determine your program's needs, begin by looking at ways to utilize and coordinate with existing resources. There's no need to reinvent the wheel, and just as a family literacy program draws from the strengths of the families, so too can it draw from the strengths in your community. Again, turn to your community assessment and answer these questions:

1. What services are being offered, by whom, and to whom?

2. Who are the key representatives in the organizations offering services to families?

3. How are similar organizations funded? What other members of your community are involved in charitable or service-based organizations?

Developing a list of potential partners does not mean that you would or should collaborate with everyone on that list—the key here is potential. As you begin to talk to representatives of various agencies throughout your community, ask questions based on the research you did prior to contacting them. The better you understand what each is trying to accomplish, the better you'll be able to assess whether they are an appropriate partner for a family literacy program. In creating collaborative partnerships, quantity is not the goal. It's better to have two or three strong, knowledgeable, committed partners than twenty partners who dodge your phone calls or are inaccessible for meetings.

[6] Winer, Michael and Ray, Karen. *Collaboration Handbook: Creating, Sustaining and Enjoying the Journey*. St. Paul, Minnesota: Amherst H. Wilder Foundation, 1994, p. 24.

When you approach organizations in your community about collaboration, be sure to approach them positively, not with the intention of "improving" their agency, but with the goal of improving services to families. Be sensitive to turf issues, and remember that implementing a family literacy program isn't a competition to see who can provide services best. It is a community endeavor to provide the best services to families.

Following is a list of potential partners, some or all of whom may be operating in your community. As you look over this list, you may think of other organizations who would be interested in your program. Research them and then call them! Forming partnerships to support your family literacy program takes creative thinking (outside the box), perseverance (but not peskiness), and impetus (go get them!)

1. A likely place to start is by focusing on the four components of comprehensive family literacy, considering ways to introduce or enhance family literacy services within existing programs. Are there agencies or organizations that work extensively in education for preschool or school-age children, adult education or parent training? These programs may embrace the opportunity to expand their services or geographical outreach, and they may already be working with many adults or children in your target population.

2. Your community may have a federally funded Even Start Family Literacy program in place. If so, the coordinator would no doubt welcome your interest. If there is not an Even Start program in your community, you may want to investigate the potential of establishing one through your state education agency. If you're not sure whether there is an Even Start program in your area, try contacting your local school district or state education agency.

3. Establish a relationship with the local and/or state department of social services, community-based services, or TANF office. The connection that your local welfare agency can provide to families at risk will prove invaluable, as will their knowledge of welfare mandates in your community. A combination of family literacy and work experience

may be a viable—and powerful—option for families moving from welfare to work. Be sure to explore all the possibilities of partnering with your local welfare office.

4. Elementary and secondary schools often provide site locations for family literacy programs, but may also have staff such as parent educators who are able to assist your program. Importantly, working with schools can help foster greater acceptance from the community; their advocacy can generate support from the community and can also help in recruiting families. (See later in this chapter for more information about collaborating with school systems.)

5. Preschool programs, including Head Start, can collaborate in referring parents, as well as in providing early childhood education and related services to families.

6. Adolescent, adult and alternative education centers may offer potential site locations, potential staff, or have staff who could serve in an advisory capacity. They may also be able to provide referrals.

7. Child care centers may be willing to coordinate services, advise your program on its child care needs, and help in the recruitment of families.

8. Many libraries have literacy or other tutoring programs in place, and are excellent at coordinating events and raising public awareness. Library staff may be willing to lead field trips or speak to classes, or there may be volunteer/work experience opportunities at the library.

9. Corporations and industries can not only provide funding, they can help you develop work-focused curriculum, can partner as potential employers for your welfare-to-work programs, and may volunteer speakers for Parent Time.

10. Immigrant and refugee agencies may provide you with referrals and help in recruitment efforts, and may be able to offer guidance or instruction for your English Language Learner (ELL) classrooms.

11. Migrant education programs can provide staff and curriculum development, as well as recruitment.

12. Workforce Investment Boards (formerly Private Industry Councils), employment "one-stop" centers, departments of labor or employment services, and employment/temporary agencies have important contacts and expertise to help with career exploration and job placement services.

13. Universities and colleges often have a vested interest in adult and community education programs, and can offer facilities or other resources (such as computer equipment), volunteers or student teachers, speakers, and professional development for staff. The Federal Work-Study (FWS) Waiver allows colleges and universities to use federal funds to pay 100% of an eligible FWS student's wages if he or she is employed in a family literacy program. An eligible FWS student may perform a variety of qualifying family literacy activities, including tutoring, training tutors, performing administrative tasks such as coordinating tutors' schedules, working as an instructional aide, or preparing family literacy materials. Further, as of July 2000, institutions are required to use 7% of the total amount of FWS funds to compensate students employed in community service activities, which includes family literacy. For more information about the FWS Waiver, visit the Web site for the Department of Education at www.ed.gov.

14. Churches and clergy may help with volunteer tutors, can aid in recruitment efforts, and may have facilities or equipment that a program can utilize.

15. Hospitals and health care centers may be able to provide speakers or volunteers, and may donate supplies or possibly services. You might also look to see if there is a local

Reach Out and Read (ROR) program in your area. Reach Out and Read is a national initiative that makes early literacy part of pediatric primary care.

16. Family support organizations or human resource agencies may be able to offer guidance in areas such as mental health, domestic violence and substance abuse, possibly providing classroom speakers.

17. In your community, there may be a prison that either provides literacy services or is interested in providing such services.

18. Professional associations and civic organizations can provide speakers, volunteer tutors, organize the donation of services, and help raise public awareness.

19. National organizations such as Literacy Volunteers of America and Laubach Literacy, and other local literacy organizations or coalitions who offer tutor and volunteer training are often essential collaborators who can help organize volunteer efforts and provide tutor support in the classroom.

20. Federal, state and local governments can provide both financial and policy support to help your program remain viable. Local officials may be looking for a mutually beneficial situation when it comes to public relations and can partner with you for special events. Everything from federal grants to community block grants could be a source of support. Be sure to check the Federal Register on a regular basis for announcements of federal support opportunities. (The Federal Register is a clearinghouse of information for federal funding that posts public announcements of federal funding sources. You can access it through the U.S. Government Printing Office's Web site at www.access.gpo.gov or through most local libraries.)

21. Local media can be a powerful ally for raising public awareness and generating interest and support in your program from community leaders and policy makers, as well as the community in general.

As you can see from the above list, which is not meant to be exhaustive, there are many different ways that partners can help you build a strong or stronger program. The most important considerations when developing a list of potential partners, as with every other aspect of implementing a family literacy program, are the needs of the families themselves. Think about the families' needs, find out who can or will or does fulfill those needs, then ask if those resources will help create or expand a family literacy program. If an organization or person can't do what you ask them to, ask them to do something else!

The School System as a Collaborative Partner

There are several reasons why working with your local schools may prove a valuable collaboration for a family literacy program. Linking to the public school system can be a beneficial partnership for your program and for the broad mission of family literacy, improving educational achievement throughout your community. Federal funding streams that typically support family literacy and related services are often channeled through public schools (for example, adult education, Even Start, preschool programs, and Reading Excellence grants.)

The existence of classrooms, supplies, and other facilities such as libraries and computer labs, makes schools a good place to house family literacy. At the same time, bear in mind that sometimes classrooms are full, supplies are short, and other facilities are optimally used.

One inherent benefit in collaborating with the school system is physically involving parents with the school that their child attends. Attending family literacy classes in the school setting can help parents overcome negative feelings they may harbor about their previous educational experiences and can help them feel more comfortable and confident in their role as supporter of their child's education. There may even be opportunities for parents to volunteer or work in the school, further integrating them into the school environment while providing them useful job experience.

There are also obvious advantages for children when family literacy programs collaborate with the school system. Preschool children gain a good introduction to the school setting which may facilitate their transition to school. For school-aged children, taking part in a family literacy program that works with their school can build on and enhance their school experiences, and can help create a positive learning atmosphere within the school setting.

Schools are often centrally located within communities to serve the greatest number of children. They may also have the ability to provide transportation or meals for participants in your family literacy program. And if you're considering collaborating with your local school system, don't forget the "win-win" relationship—for schools, they may especially be attracted to the opportunity to access additional funds from new sources such as adult education or parental involvement programs in support of family literacy. Remember though, as you approach your local school system, there may be some hesitancy to embrace the adult education component of family literacy, not because the schools are opposed to it but because adult education may be unfamiliar territory. Many schools focus on K-12 education. Be fully versed in how adult education is provided in your community and state, and in how local schools may collaborate with adult education providers.

The Community-Based Organization as a Collaborative Partner

There may be situations where a school is not the most appropriate, convenient or logical collaborative partner. The first order of business, again, is looking at what is going to serve families best. Part of that consideration is looking at where families are most likely to use services.

There are several advantages to partnering with a community-based organization (CBO), the first of which is its very nature. Community-based implies that the organization has strong ties to the community—and further, that these ties are reciprocal (staff are connected to the community, and the community is aware of and comfortable with the staff and the organization.) Physically, a CBO often has a widely accessible facility located within the community, and may have systems in place to reach families in need.

A CBO usually has the trust of the community, and parents may be more at ease in a community center setting than they are in a school setting. Similarly, CBOs may have staff in place who are respected in the community, particularly by your target population, and can work as "gatekeepers" in your recruitment efforts. Along these same lines, CBOs may be particularly effective at getting the word out to the community and raising public awareness of its programs.

Another benefit to collaborating with a CBO is that it may already be providing services to families in need, services that family literacy can build on. And as a service organization, and usually a nonprofit one at that, a CBO is often accustomed to working in collaborative ventures. In fact, it may already be working with some of the other agencies and organizations that are on your potential partner list.

Are there other options besides partnering with a school system or community-based organization? Of course. Do you have to partner with a school system or community-based organization? No. These are just two potentially useful allies for your family literacy program, and will be a good place to start as you begin to explore all of the collaborative opportunities in your community.

Making Contact

The only way to evaluate interest in and garner support for your program is to talk to people—preferably key representatives within the various agencies, organizations and businesses that you've identified as potential partners. While it may seem a little time consuming, you should speak with each potential partner individually first, rather than starting out with a group meeting of all your potential partners. You will want to make sure that every partner is a good "fit" with your program, and you will need to provide potential partners pertinent information to help them decide if your program is an appropriate "fit" for them as well.

While it's ideal to carefully research and investigate all potential partners in your community, realistically a program developer may be responding to a specific Request for Proposal (RFP) or other funding opportunity. This may mean that you do not have a lot of time to go from agency to agency, as you may be working to write a proposal within a short time frame. Remember, though, that collaborative partnerships are not static—they need continual evaluation and maintenance, just like a family literacy program itself. When establishing new partnerships, and again under ideal circumstances, budget at least six months to nurture and build the partnership into a solid, mutual, working relationship.

Good communication starts with listening. After you have gathered as much basic information as you can about potential partners through their publications, discuss with your contact or another representative exactly what the purpose of the organization is, how it operates, and what the organization's interest is in education or family services. You may find out right off the bat that the organization's goals are at cross-purposes with the goals you have in mind at this point. That probably isn't very likely, but again, the emphasis on establishing partnerships is quality, not quantity, and it's okay if some potential partners turn out to be inappropriate or, in some cases, not useful. It's better to identify that at the start than to put effort into an ineffective collaboration.

Once you've determined which partners are worth pursuing, come to the first meeting with a potential partner with information about family literacy (either developed by your program, or publications from an organization such as NCFL that illustrate the effectiveness of the family literacy educational approach). Be prepared to tell potential partners your vision of family literacy in your community and how that applies to what their organizations or agencies do. In the early stages, as you're working to establish new partnerships, you may present your vision in terms of your community assessment (what the community does and doesn't provide for families in need) and your goals (how a family literacy program will help families receive the services they need). How do the goals of the program match the expectations of the potential partner? Also, be prepared to provide a concise overview of family literacy—people won't be eager to support something they don't understand.

As you talk with potential partners, you may be tempted to tailor your vision to fit what you think they want to hear, to make yourself a more attractive collaborator. This is dangerous. First of all, you've pursued the idea of a family literacy program based on the families in your community, and their goals won't change just because you've changed your vision. Also, if you adjust your vision with every potential collaborative partner you meet, you run the risk of blurring your vision with convoluted messages and your program will lose its focus. The program, and your vision, must always focus on the strengths and needs of families as you try to raise support for your program.

Once you've begun to establish a relationship with each individual agency and organization, it is crucial to gather all of your potential partners together. Representatives from each may serve as members of a planning or steering committee for the family literacy program. While you plan for this to be the first of many meetings, assure potential partners that their time will be respected and the meeting will stick to a specific agenda and time period (and this should certainly be true of all subsequent meetings, too).

The first meeting should focus on creating a common mission for family literacy in your community (see information later in this chapter on creating a mission statement). It will take time for all partners to work through the complex process of collaborating on providing services to families—but it's well worth it! In a series of meetings, your partners and you will identify the goals of both the program and the collaborative and the responsibilities of each partner, to be sure that you are not duplicating efforts or excluding services. Your challenge is to build a collaborative team that will be able to guide the program at every level. Think in terms of what you can accomplish as a group that you cannot accomplish individually. This takes time, patience, an open mind, and constant focus on the families of your community.

Getting everyone to agree is not always easy. Be clear about what family literacy is and what it takes to make it work, and why it is the most effective approach to working with your target population. It's all right—even necessary—to compromise when working in a collaboration, as long as you don't lose the focus on the "family" in family literacy. You may have partners who are more interested in or capable of working with adult education or children's education, but you are building a program that works with adults and children together, and that ideology must stay in the forefront of your program development.

Also, within these first steps of collaboration, it's critical to decide who will be the coordinating or lead agency for the program. While you should work to honor all collaborative partners' ideas and goals equally, there should be one agency whose ultimate responsibility is to actually make the program happen—to get the program open and keep it open.

As you're talking with potential collaborators, also keep in mind that they may lead you to new potential collaborators who aren't on your list. Once you've established your network of collaborative partners, continuously seek their input on attracting other collaborative partners for the future. Fresh perspectives are always helpful!

Making it Official

Potential partners are usually much more comfortable with informal agreements during the early stages of a partnership. Follow-up letters thanking them for agreeing to send out your materials in their mailings, for example, may be sufficient documentation at first. Keeping informal collaborators informed on how their agency has helped the program progress, especially in areas where their agency documents outcomes, will make a formal agreement easier to reach.

At the appropriate time, you should adopt some sort of formal agreement so that responsibilities are clearly defined. Again, working out all these details will take time. The answers to the questions listed below will develop over the course of several meetings with your partners once the program's vision, mission and goals are established.

1. Who will be the lead agency of the program? Who will be in charge of program coordination, either at a single site or among several sites? There should be only one agency charged with the responsibility of program coordination.

2. Who will be the lead fiscal agency? There most likely will be multiple streams of funding, but there should only be one agency who is responsible for tracking, recording and reporting fiscal information.

3. Who will be responsible for reporting program activities (financially and otherwise) to funders and other partners?

4. How often will you and your partners meet to discuss your program's progress? What other ways can you ensure an active, reciprocal partnership? What are the criteria for pursuing future collaborative partners?

As you develop partnerships, keep a record of your collaborative efforts so you can evaluate them and make needed improvements. Some of the areas to address are:

1. How did the collaboration begin?

2. Who is a member and why?

3. What does each member give and get?

4. What resources and personnel are you sharing within the program?

5. What benefits does your agency or group receive by being part of the collaborative effort?

6. What successes have been achieved by the collaboration?

7. What improvements can be made in the collaboration?

8. What do you see in the future?

It might be interesting (and informative) for you to ask all your partners to answer the previous questions, and then compare those answers. You may find that different partners identify different strengths and benefits.

Keeping collaborative partners, including funders, informed and enthusiastic about the program and family literacy in general is critical to maintaining good relationships. You may wish to establish an advisory board that includes members from your collaborative partners, as well as other key community leaders or experts in related fields, to provide guidance on program issues from advocacy to troubleshooting to staff policies. Always keep partners informed, share your successes, and keep a record of the benefits your partners receive as a result of their connection with the program. Find out what your partners need and want in terms of assessments of the program's progress, and how involved they expect to be in day-to-day activities. Always invite them to special events (but never demand that they attend), give them the opportunity to go on site visits, and provide them with opportunities to receive media coverage of their involvement with your program (if they desire it). Always credit them in any written materials about the program (unless they specifically request to remain anonymous). Provide them the data they require, but also share with them the stories of the families in the program—the more connected they are to the program, the more effective they'll be as partners!

The Mission Statement

Your community assessment and your established partnerships (including funding sources) are a great foundation for building a family literacy program. Before getting into the meat and potatoes of program design, there's another step that will help you build a program based on the goals and interests of your target population: developing a mission statement.

Thanks to your community assessment and the many interviews you've conducted with other service organizations and agencies, you probably have a good grasp on who your target population is—most likely those who demonstrate the most urgent needs.

While you don't want to define them so narrowly as to exclude anyone from receiving the services they need, it is necessary to be specific about your target population in order to form your mission statement and to clarify the program's goals. You don't want a target population that is defined so broadly that your program's vision loses its focus or that you try to offer so many services that none reaches families effectively.

The identifying factors of your target population will probably be defined in some clear way, such as by geographical borders, by school district, or by a connection to one local employer. There may be other factors that help you select the parameters of your target population, such as the availability of a central location and accessibility to that location. Your collaborative partners may also be looking to serve families with particular goals or characteristics, or who live in a particular geographic area. Consider those families that you want to reach, that you can reach, and that you can reach most effectively. Think, too, about the impact this target population's economic and educational challenges have on your community at large.

Your program's mission statement will help you refine your message, which can be used to describe the program and its benefits to potential funders, other agencies and organizations, staff, and families. The mission statement should identify the need for a family literacy program in your community by addressing the needs of your target population. By defining your target population, you may indicate that existing services aren't meeting the needs of that population (e.g., "families in which parents lack basic skills, are unemployed or employed in low-wage jobs, and consequently whose children are at high risk of academic failure"). The mission statement should also describe how the program will meet those needs (e.g., "by providing intense and sustained instruction to adults and children together, our organization will work to provide opportunities for parents to improve basic skills, obtain a job and move forward on a career path, and increase the academic achievement of at-risk children").

That's a lot of information to fit into one brief statement! At the same time, your program's mission should be as clear and concise as possible so that it can be used as a powerful communication tool for a variety of audiences. Likewise, the mission statement should be broad in scope, so as not to preclude growth. Remember that a mission statement is just that—a statement, not an essay. It should be no more than one sentence.

You will revise your mission statement (probably more than once) as you and your collaborative partners learn more about the families you work with. If possible, the program's staff should also contribute to the construction of the mission statement. Remember that the families' needs and goals—not the program's abilities—should be the focus of your mission.

Funding Considerations

We might as well admit it: starting and maintaining a family literacy program costs money. How much money depends on numerous factors that are determined by the individual structure of your program within your community. But just as there are multiple parts of a family literacy program that must be paid for, there are multiple sources from whom you may seek funding—federal, state and local resources, private funding, local businesses and national businesses, civic organizations, and individuals. Explore them all!

The basic funding streams you'll most likely encounter fall into two very broad categories: public and private. Many family literacy programs blend funds from both these categories. There are dollars available through federal government funding, particularly through the legislation that includes the consistent federal definition of family literacy services (Head Start Act, Elementary and Secondary Education Act [Title I Parts A and B], Community Services Block Grants, Reading Excellence Act, and the Adult Education and Family Literacy Act). Much of this funding is distributed to State Education Agencies (SEAs), who then distribute the funds locally to Local Education Agencies (LEAs). Many states also have other funds that they allocate to adult education, children's education, or family literacy initiatives.

Private funding generally comes from foundations, corporations and individual donors. There are many foundations and corporations interested in supporting valid, effective educational programs, and they usually offer funding through grants for which an agency or organization applies. Sometimes these grants are made available to explore or enhance a particular realm of education, such as strategies for helping parents transition from welfare to work, and sometimes they can offer general operating support. Often private funding sources are interested in programs or initiatives in a specific geographic location, either a state or a city, or those that serve a particular population.

The most important step in securing funding is research. You don't want to waste your time—or a potential donor's time—in applying for a grant that you're not eligible for, or by not supplying all of the information that a Request for Proposal or grant application requires. Some ways to research potential giving sources are through corporate annual reports, public relations staff members, corporate contributions history, the business section of your local paper, Chamber of Commerce directories, business magazines, the Federal Register (available on-line at www.access.gpo.gov and through libraries), and the Internet. Always, always, read application guidelines carefully, and provide all—but *only*—the information they require.

Bear in mind as you begin this part of your family literacy journey that you will need to have a financial plan in place from the start, a way that you will record all of your fiscal activity. You will be held accountable by all your funders, as well as other collaborative partners, for all of your expenses. For government funding, you will be required to document the proper use of funds and have audits conducted. Be sure that you understand all of the requirements of documentation for each source of funding. If you're not experienced in finances, solicit the help of someone who is.

It is also critical to think right now—before you put down this guide!—about the future, or sustainability, of your family literacy program. It's not enough to plan how to open a program. You must plan from the beginning how to keep a program open and maintain it for many years. How will you not only keep funders satisfied with your program's current progress, but assure them of future progress so that they will continue to invest? How will you attract new funders and for what purposes (e.g., to improve program technology, to increase staff development opportunities)? How can you make the most of start-up funding to map out fiscal security for the future? If one element of your financial plan falls through, what other resources do you have available to fill in gaps? This forward thinking carries over to all your collaborative partnerships. Make it part of your strategic plan to continuously improve the delivery of services to families through interagency collaboration and find ways to keep all your partnerships effective and productive.

One last word on collaboration: the best way to raise money and other resources, attract new collaborative partners, and garner the support of your community is to speak about the program to anyone who'll listen—civic and professional organizations, legislative gatherings, town meetings, school board meetings, religious gatherings, and so forth. Be sure that your mission is clear, and people will share your enthusiasm for family literacy and promote it to other members of your community. Once your family literacy program is under way, you'll also find that your students make great speakers for groups. No one expresses the success of a family literacy program better than someone who has lived it.

Chapter 4:
Program Design and Anticipated Outcomes

Program Design Fundamentals

With a thorough community assessment that identifies the need for family literacy services in your area, a resourceful group of collaborative partners ready to share their expertise, and funding in place, it's time now to consider the very practical issues involved in establishing and maintaining a comprehensive family literacy program.

The process of designing a quality family literacy program is extremely complex, involving multiple disciplines, diligent planning, committed teamwork, keen organizational and communication skills, and lots of patience and positive thinking! Ultimately, the object of program design is to create and maintain the most effective program possible, one that serves an optimum number of families in an efficient, relevant, and dynamic way.

Good program design takes:

- Planning
- Teamwork
- Organization
- Communication
- Patience
- Positive thinking

There are several purposes to thoughtful and careful program design:

1. To ensure the smooth delivery of services (both educational and non-educational) that address the goals of the program and the goals of the families.

2. To continuously improve the quality and impact of your program through staff development, technical assistance and evaluation.

3. To facilitate ongoing collaborations with other agencies, organizations, businesses and the community to guarantee the longevity of your program.

In order to develop an effective program design that achieves these three purposes, planning must be a continual process before, during and after you open the doors to your program. The following chapters will focus on the three major areas of program design:

1. **Anticipated Outcomes.** Determining the program's anticipated outcomes is the starting point for program design. The results you expect to achieve will give the program it's overall shape, and will strongly influence the other two areas of program design.

2. **Elements of Design**. These elements consist of such practical requirements as staffing, site location, preliminary scheduling, and coordinating other services such as meals, transportation and off-site child care—all the day-to-day considerations for running a family literacy program efficiently and sensitively to meet the needs of the participants.

3. **Strategies**. The best way to ensure the future of the program is to plan for it! You'll want to implement ways to keep the program running smoothly and to continually improve its effectiveness with strategies such as staff development, evaluation, recruitment and retention, and building public awareness and community support.

A Note About Evaluation

We will reiterate this sentiment several times throughout this guide: *Key to the success of a family literacy program is having an evaluation plan in place from the very beginning.* Evaluation provides the information needed to make decisions—decisions that will affect your anticipated outcomes, the elements you utilize to run the program effectively, your communication with collaborative partners (including funders), and of course, the students.

From the start, not only do you need to have an evaluation plan, you need to determine who or what agency will be responsible for making sure that data is routinely collected and your evaluation plan is carried out. The evaluation plan should be developed jointly by the staff who are involved in the everyday operation of the program as well as all of the collaborative agencies to ensure that it will evaluate all the necessary areas (including both learner outcomes and program outcomes).

For these reasons, evaluation needs to be among your first thoughts in designing a family literacy program, even though much of the actual evaluation process will not occur until the program is up and running. Because the evaluation process will help you keep the program relevant and perpetually improving, it will be discussed more at length in the "Strategies for Success" chapter.

Before We Get Started

Like the four components of family literacy, the features of program design will be integrated to form a strong, cohesive and comprehensive design. Each feature will impact other features, and will have to be considered in the larger context of the overall design—the big picture—to reach maximum effectiveness. We've said it before, but we can't resist saying it again: good program design takes good planning. The information that follows in this and subsequent chapters will help you organize your team's efforts so that everyone is working in tandem to create the strongest program possible.

Anticipated Outcomes

Through your community assessment, you've determined that there is a need for a comprehensive, quality family literacy program in your area. Your collaborative partners are on board and are ready to take the next steps. Funds have been secured, or at least identified. You've crafted a powerful mission statement and defined your target population. So, what—specifically—do you think a family literacy program can and will accomplish for those at-risk families that your assessment has identified?

Answering this question is the first step in developing a family literacy program design. But don't answer it alone. As you read further in this chapter, be sure to think of ways to involve all your staff in the process of setting goals and anticipated outcomes. (Staff selection is discussed in the next chapter.)

Clear goal statements are an important part of family literacy—they will give the program direction and purpose and will guide practices in and outside the classroom. Goals for the program should be broad enough to allow for adjustment, particularly when the individual goals of each of the families are identified. In general, the sample goals stated below offer both an outline to help you focus and room to allow program growth. Consider these as a starting point.

Sample Program Goals:

- Improve basic skills and/or English language skills of parents so that they may be better prepared to support their child's education

- Raise the employability skills of adults to foster economic stability for the family

- Increase the likelihood for academic success of children by promoting parental involvement through the educational attainment of parents

---

- Improve parenting skills and enhance parent-child relationships in order to increase support systems in vulnerable families

- Coordinate services to families to increase the effectiveness of those services

Goals should be stated in a way that provides room to address the individual goals of the families your program serves.

Once the goals are in place, it's time to tackle specific outcomes. Deciding what your specific outcomes are going to be before you've set up your program can seem a little like guessing your team's final score in the Super Bowl before you've held the first scrimmage. At the same time, sometimes it's easier to see a path when you've already determined where your desired destination is. Setting general goals for a family literacy program will help you take the first steps down the program design path. Formulating anticipated outcomes for achievements within the components of your program will help you plan the necessary steps to meet and exceed those goals and outcomes. Anticipated outcomes will also provide a tool to help you describe the program to potential participants, and can be used to help students begin identifying specific short- and long-term goals and ways to achieve them.

Outcomes are part of a three-part framework for design that also includes strategies for program processes and evaluation. Each of these elements are equally important. Without strategies and evaluation, outcomes will be difficult to achieve and assess.

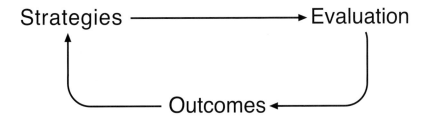

While you and your staff are creating anticipated outcomes, keep in mind the next steps. Clearly defining outcomes will help determine the strategies—both general program design elements and classroom instruction—needed to achieve those outcomes. And you will need to choose evaluation methods and instruments that assess whether or not the outcomes are being achieved. Remember too that throughout the goal-setting process students will play a key role in determining their individual goals, which will affect anticipated outcomes, strategies and evaluation.

Purposes of Determining Outcomes

There are many reasons to set goals and commit to anticipated outcomes for a family literacy program and for the families enrolled. First and foremost, you, the program staff, and all of your collaborators must have a strong, common vision of what your family literacy program intends to do and how it intends to do it. It's always easier and more productive to work together toward specific achievements rather than working against multiple cross-purposes.

You will also want to define the role your program will play in the community and how you will be able to serve families in a way that no other existing service does. This is useful both in making your case to the community for support and to families for recruitment. Stating clearly what you expect a family literacy program to accomplish, including what gaps in services it will fill, will help you rally supporters and build enthusiasm among potential participants. Remember that family literacy can be a difficult "concept" to grasp—anticipated outcomes may be the most easily understood or tangible part of family literacy. They will help you communicate how family literacy will benefit families specifically and the community in general.

Setting your program goals and anticipated outcomes will help you to begin analyzing the essential elements of your program like staffing requirements, budget considerations and other practical concerns that are necessary to get the program on its feet. As you're formulating your anticipated outcomes, keep a list of potential resources that occur to you—these can help you plan your strategies for program design and can also play into recruitment efforts.

You will want to have in place from the start an evaluation plan that 1) identifies and clarifies families' progress toward achieving their goals; 2) measures progress toward achieving program goals; and 3) informs the planning and delivery of your curriculum. Some of your evaluation methods will be determined by your anticipated outcomes. The reverse of that, though, is also true: considering methods of evaluation can help you focus anticipated outcomes. For example, examining GED competencies may help you formulate initial outcomes for the adult education component of your family literacy program (keeping in mind, always, that the outcomes for enrolled families must reflect the goals that the families set for themselves). The value of evaluation to inform all of the practices in a family literacy program is often overlooked, especially in these initial stages of design, but it is an integral part of the entire family literacy process.

As you begin to consider anticipated outcomes for your family literacy program, be sure to continually refer to your community assessment. Remember that your program is intended to fill in the gaps that other services don't already provide, for the population most in need in your community. The object of determining anticipated outcomes is to look at how family literacy programs uniquely help families develop their own strategies for lifelong learning, employability, parenting and creating a successful future for children. Also, it bears repeating, be sure that your anticipated outcomes take into account the cultural diversity of the population you wish to serve. The power of family literacy is that programs draw on the unique strengths of families and build on goals that are relevant to their individual circumstances.

> *Remember that your program is intended to fill in the gaps that other services don't already provide.*

One word of warning: be sure to honestly consider the reality of your anticipated outcomes. While you don't want to limit the program, or especially the families in the program, you also don't want to set such broad or numerous outcomes that the task at hand is intimidating, overwhelming or impossible. Think about what outcomes are short-term, and what outcomes might be more suitable for the long-term. Be ambitious but practical about the expectations you have for the program.

Types of Outcomes

There are three primary areas of a family literacy program that you will want to examine when formulating your anticipated outcomes: Participant Outcomes, Program Outcomes and Continuous Improvement Strategies.

Before you get started formulating your anticipated outcomes, one excellent resource to study is the *Even Start Guide to Quality*. This guide offers succinct descriptions of quality indicators for Even Start programs in such areas as "Integration of Components," "Recruitment" and "Staff Development," and also includes a program self-assessment tool.[7] Also, many state education agencies have or are developing performance indicators for family literacy programs through federally funded statewide family literacy grants. And don't forget your collaborative partners—they may be accountable for particular outcomes by way of their own funding sources.

Participant Outcomes

Most of your program's anticipated outcomes will be framed by the four components of family literacy—adult education, children's education, Parent Time, and Parent and Child Together (PACT) Time. It is within these four components—and through integration across the components—that you will work directly with families to help them achieve their educational and non-educational goals. Your program's anticipated outcomes in this area may be very generalized for now; however, you may think in terms of the highest priorities

---

[7] Prepared by M. Christine Dwyer, RMC Research Corporation, Portsmouth, NH, for Even Start Program, Office of Compensatory Education, U.S. Department of Education, 1998.

within your target population and focus on outcomes that will help participants reach their most urgent goals.

Following are some considerations for you to think about as you begin to develop family outcomes within each of the components. At the end of this section are some broad sample outcomes from NCFL initiatives that may help guide you in determining anticipated outcomes for participants who enroll in your program. Be sure also to check with your state education agencies to see if statewide outcomes for family literacy have been identified. Also, clarify any accountability issues with your collaborative partners.

Outcomes for Adults

Adult learners' specific goals may range from completing their high school education to increasing their employability skills to improving their English language skills. Adults in family literacy programs, who often represent the nation's most impoverished populations, may suffer from poor health, have domestic violence issues, may not be able to afford adequate child care, or may not have transportation. They may lack vocational skills or they may need more help in improving "soft skills" like communication and problem solving. There also may be other social or personal pressures that adult learners are facing that you're not aware of or that are beyond your control.

Adults are individuals. Adult learners are individuals, too. The parents and caregivers who enroll in a family literacy program may be looking for accomplishment in the workplace, at home, or in some other way. Only that parent or caregiver knows in what area he or she most wants or needs to improve, and it's important to honor that. It is also important to help expand the view of adults who may feel their potential is limited based on their past experiences, their income, or the accumulation of unfulfilled dreams.

In a family literacy program, adult education classes center around the students' lives and goals, educational and non-educational, and you may have to be creative in making your program as accessible and productive as possible for each adult learner. Adults are more motivated to learn when the instruction is individualized based on personal and academic goals. In helping adults determine their own goals, you help them recognize their existing strengths.

Family literacy also stresses facilitating the application of skills and knowledge in real life settings, rather than teaching stand-alone skills. The very nature of the four components supports this application. The opportunity to immediately put new knowledge into practice can be especially appealing to adult learners, who are facing "real life" challenges constantly. As you're thinking about potential outcomes for families, consider ways to make the learning opportunities "real" for parents and caregivers.

You may want to explore competencies of certain standardized tests and frameworks like the GED (for educational competencies), CASAS (life skills), SCANS (workplace skills) or TESOL (for ESL students) to get other ideas about anticipated outcomes for the adult education component of your program (for information about these specific assessments, see NCFL's publication *Outcomes and Measures*). There may be particular state or federal requirements that your anticipated outcomes should address. Also, you may want to look at the *Equipped for the Future Content Standards* for suggestions about working with adults in their roles as workers, citizens, and parents/family members (available through the Web site of the National Institute for Literacy at www.nifl.gov, or through the EDPUBS Clearinghouse of the U.S. Department of Education at 1-877-4-ED-PUBS).

Particularly affecting the adults in your programs are issues surrounding welfare reform and achieving economic independence. Be sure you consider how welfare reform is affecting your community and especially what requirements adults must meet as you determine anticipated goals for the adult education components.

Outcomes for Children

In its early years, family literacy concentrated on providing education for parents and their preschool-aged children. But as the family literacy movement grew, so too did its reach, and programs are now expanding to include families with infants and toddlers as well as school-aged children.

The anticipated outcomes of the children's education component will depend on the ages and developmental stages of the children you expect to enroll in the program, and this may in part be determined not only by your particular community but also by the purposes of your partners and collaborators. While you don't want to deter families with children of different ages from attending the program, you will want to consider how the program is best going to serve those families. Again, your most valuable tool in determining the type of children's education your program will offer is your community assessment, which can be used to entice appropriate children's education partners. The children's education component, like the other three essential components of family literacy, will be built on the needs and strengths of the families.

For children of any age, attention to literacy development is primary. You will also want to look at ways of encouraging the physical, behavioral and intellectual development of the children enrolled in your program. Remember that children, like adults, will possess different levels of development and will require individualized instruction.

It may also be appropriate for you to consider what parents say their children's strengths and interests are, and what parents want for their children. Parents are the leaders of their families. It's no accident that parents are included in three of the four components in family literacy—that is certainly not to discount the value of the children's education component, but to emphasize the importance of integration of children's education with the other components.

Resources that might identify outcomes for the children's education component will be determined by the age of the children that the program will reach. Potential sources include the local school district, a local Head Start agency, and the National Association for the Education of Young Children (NAEYC). Remember to consider also how welfare mandates affect families and how, in turn, this affects the children who will enroll in the program. Your curriculum, even in the children's education component, may partially need to address the transitions experienced by families new to the world of work.

Outcomes for Parent Time

Parent Time is a regularly planned class where adults work on skills that support their most important role as parents. The many topics discussed during Parent Time offer adults the opportunity to connect basic skills to their "real life" situations, using communication, problem solving and critical thinking skills through practical applications. Central to Parent Time is helping parents understand and support their children's literacy skills development.

It's important to note that Parent Time focuses on learning. Most teachers are not trained therapists and should be cautious especially when dealing with difficult issues that may be more suitably addressed by another professional. While Parent Time does offer a forum for adults to discuss key issues with one another, the emphasis of Parent Time is on improving skills and expanding the learning experience.

There are three primary purposes for Parent Time, and the outcomes you develop will reflect these:

1. *Sharing of information and new ideas to improve and increase parenting skills.* Parent Time supports parents' roles as their children's first teacher by building their awareness of child development, especially the development of literacy skills in children. This component also offers adults the opportunity to discuss other issues that affect

the well-being of the family and which directly or indirectly impact children's literacy development, such as health care and nutrition, family economics, legal rights, and school procedures and expectations.

2. *Sharing encouragement and peer support.* Many impoverished adults experience isolation, anxiety and hopelessness. Having a consistent group of supporters with whom to discuss real problems and brainstorm solutions can help adults find strengths within themselves to take a more active part in their lives and the lives of their children. Working in a team or group setting also helps to improve listening and communicating skills.

3. *Providing advocacy and referrals to other services.* Some of the issues adults in family literacy programs face are beyond the scope and expertise of in-house staff. At times, it may be necessary to refer parents to other services available to them, such as legal assistance, counseling or therapy, housing assistance, emergency shelter, or substance abuse treatment. Parent Time offers adults the chance to learn more about these services so that they can take better advantage of them.

A well-structured Parent Time can promote group dynamics, interaction, participation, respect for personal and cultural differences, self-esteem, and critical thinking, among other things. Most teachers are not trained therapists, it's true—but all are trained facilitators. Parent Time can be an effective way to bridge the gap between classroom and "real life" circumstances.

Especially in the Parent Time component, keep in mind that change in one family member will likely have an effect on all family members. As you think about potential outcomes for Parent Time, think about how these outcomes will affect the rest of the family, as well as how the other three components in your program will affect the instruction for Parent Time.

Also as you're planning your outcomes for Parent Time, you may want to begin preparing a directory of community resources, such as community speakers who might be willing to come to your classroom and speak with students. This directory could also identify appropriate agencies for referrals. This could become a project that you work on with your students throughout the school year.

Outcomes for Parent and Child Together (PACT) Time

PACT Time is one of the hardest concepts of family literacy to grasp, especially for people outside the family literacy field. It is also the component that sets family literacy programs apart from other literacy services, so its intentions, or anticipated outcomes, must be very clear. Knowing and understanding what you expect to gain in regularly scheduled interaction time for parents and children will not only make the component stronger but will also make it easier to communicate the value of PACT Time to others, including the families themselves.

At times you may feel that you have to justify the inclusion of the PACT Time component to outsiders and to parents. PACT Time can have multiple purposes, but the primary purpose, in conjunction with Parent Time, is to assist parents in their role as their children's primary teacher. Parent Time provides the knowledge base; PACT Time offers practice time for parenting skills. And there are many ways that PACT Time does this.

Regularly scheduled and professionally facilitated interaction time provides parents the opportunity to practice new techniques in a safe, supportive environment where teachers can model learning strategies and offer suggestions. By providing concrete examples, PACT Time can enhance a parent's awareness of how children learn, and can provide tools and techniques to support children's learning in the home. PACT Time can also help build a parent's interest in the child's learning process and motivate families to carry that process from the classroom into the home and through the rest of their lives. So, while PACT Time works to strengthen parenting skills, it is imbued by a deeper purpose of building a family foundation for learning.

PACT Time also offers group activities which are led by staff to support the transfer of literacy activities to the home. These activities are usually reviewed in Parent Time or in the Adult Education classroom to further assist parents in understanding and implementing solid home learning behaviors.

As mentioned earlier, you may encounter some resistance at first from parents who do not immediately recognize the benefits of interacting with their children or feel uncomfortable in the PACT Time setting. As you consider your anticipated outcomes for this component, you may also want to think about how you will help foster positive feelings in parents toward their children's learning and toward their participation in that learning. Also keep in mind that you will need to document this component, just as you do all the others. How will this component be evaluated? What specific skills can you identify in parents and children as they interact and how can you measure their progress in developing these skills?

PACT Time can also be a fun time for parents and children to play together, and there is a message in that as well—that families discover how much fun learning can be. But it's important, in terms of providing the most effective quality family literacy services, that PACT Time be treated with the same seriousness and commitment that the other components receive as you're planning and maintaining your program. Involving your staff, collaborative partners, and enrolled families in determining anticipated outcomes for PACT Time can help them recognize the power of this component.

Component Integration

The strength of comprehensive family literacy is in reciprocal learning that continually reinforces new knowledge in the family—a mutual learning support system built between parents and children. This happens best when the four components are viewed as one integrated program, not stand-alone elements that happen to involve members of the same family.

Activities in each component should complement one another, which will make the whole program stronger. The only way to do this is to make team planning an integral part of your overall program. To be most effective, schedule team planning at least weekly, as part of paid staff time. You will be able to begin practicing teamwork as you develop your anticipated outcomes for the four components; work with all the members of your staff as you determine outcomes to ensure that everyone, from the start, is working towards the same, integrated purposes.

What follows are two sample listings of anticipated outcomes prepared for programs developed by the National Center for Family Literacy. These outcomes are described in very general terms, as both programs encompass multiple program sites in locations throughout the country. Your state or local agency and/or collaborative partners may require more specific anticipated outcomes that address behaviors, assessment and time periods.

Family Independence Initiative: Sample Family Outcomes

(The Family Independence Initiative, funded by the John S. and James L. Knight Foundation, looks at ways to adapt existing family literacy program models to better meet the demands of welfare legislation)

Adult Education

1. Improve reading, writing and math skills
2. Improve English language skills
3. Apply basic skills in the context of work
4. Develop/improve employability/workplace skills
5. Get a job, retain a job, or get a better job

Children's Education

1. Increase cognitive abilities, especially language and literacy
2. Improve use of English language
3. Increase social competence
4. Develop/improve fine and gross motor abilities
5. Improve self-regulatory behaviors

Parent Time

1. Increase knowledge of their child's literacy development and application of their roles as teachers of their children: modeling literacy practices, appropriate ways of supporting children's learning, etc.
2. Increase knowledge of children's development, abilities, strengths and needs
3. Increase knowledge of different approaches to discipline and behavior management of children
4. Increase knowledge of school expectations
5. Learn and practice life and family management skills

PACT Time

1. Increase quality and quantity of time spent reading, writing, talking, playing with and listening to children
2. Display positive attitudes towards children
3. Communicate positively and effectively with children
4. Apply knowledge of children's development and behavior management techniques
5. Use routine interactions with children in school and home to encourage learning and language development

Toyota Families in Schools Program: Sample Family Outcomes

(The Toyota Families in Schools Program is working to bring about fundamental changes in the interaction between schools and the parents of students from low-income families. This program works specifically with parents and elementary school-aged children.)

Adult Education
1. Set family, academic and career goals
2. Develop plans to acquire family, academic, and career goals
3. Improve academic skills
4. Improve English language skills: speaking, listening and understanding, reading and writing
5. Apply acquired and improved skills to meet daily life needs
6. Improve interpersonal/communication skills
7. Develop and utilize critical thinking skills and problem solving strategies
8. Acquire lifelong learning strategies to self-direct and monitor learning
9. Acquire knowledge of career options and their requirements
10. Develop and/or improve employability skills

Children's Education
1. Develop appropriate (age, grade, developmental) skills in all academic areas
2. Maintain a good school attendance record
3. Develop and display a positive attitude towards all aspects of school and learning
4. Develop self-discipline and positive self-esteem
5. Improve communication skills with peers and adults

Parent Time
1. Increase knowledge of child's literacy development
2. Increase understanding of the child's abilities and achievement, strengths, and weaknesses
3. Increase awareness of their role as the primary teacher of their child
4. Increase understanding of the school curriculum as it applies to their child
5. Serve as a powerful advocate for their child
6. Increase awareness and utilization of effective behavior management skills
7. Increase effective written and oral communication with the school
8. Expand support networks

PACT Time
1. Increase the quality and quantity of literacy related activities between parent and child
2. Increase the quality and quantity of parent-child play activities
3. Develop and utilize parent-child communication skills
4. Apply knowledge of child development and behavior management skills
5. Encourage language development and learning in the home and at school

Anticipated Program Outcomes

Unfortunately, there is no magic formula for structuring a family literacy program—except, of course, the inherent structure of the four components and their integration. From the physical features of programs such as facilities and equipment, to the scheduling of program activities that meet the needs of the families, to the infrastructure of a program's collaborative relationship, there are many practical considerations in the design of a comprehensive family literacy program.

How much time you schedule for each component, for team planning, how many days your program meets, how many months your program meets—these are questions that only you and your partners can answer. But the first question you must answer is: what's best for the families? The next question, in considering anticipated program outcomes, is: how can the program best help families achieve their goals?

First, be realistic in connecting anticipated outcomes for families and the program to the actual time necessary to achieve those outcomes. One hour a week in an adult education class will most likely not result in increasing an adult's literacy skills by three grade levels in a timely manner.

Federal law qualifies the definition of family literacy services as those "that are of sufficient intensity in terms of hours, and of sufficient duration, to make sustainable changes in a family." The definition of "sufficient" hinges on the goals of the families you serve and the outcomes you have established for the program overall. The "intensity" of services offered should match the intensity of need.

In considering that intensity, remember that you will need to allow enough time to balance your work in the four components as well as ample time for team planning. A family literacy program should be focused, planned, and frequent. Most programs meet between two and four days a week, and hours of operation may have to accommodate parents' work schedules or other commitments. Obviously, if the children in your program are of school-age, scheduling may have to revolve around the school day. Many programs provide home visits as well as center-based services to help maintain the "intensity" of services. The duration of most programs spans eight to nine months, and a majority of programs follow a traditional school year.

Depending on their goals, families may stay enrolled for more than one program year. The families in family literacy programs have many distracting issues in their lives. It's possible that your program will require more intensity and longer duration than other services and educational programs in your community.

There are the physical necessities of operating a family literacy program that are relatively self-evident, such as the site location, transportation, classroom materials, and possibly providing meals. All of these will have to be in place before you open your doors, and arrangements must be made carefully and thoroughly so as to avoid any unexpected breakdown in the delivery of services. Quick fixes in any of these areas could result in disorganized, inconsistent or intermittent interaction with families, which defeats the purpose of quality family literacy programs "of sufficient intensity…and of sufficient duration."

There are also operational requirements that apply to the content and process of your program design that you will need to consider, particularly as they influence your anticipated outcomes. How will your program focus on family strengths, goal setting and planning? How will you work with families on attaining their educational and non-educational goals? How will you allow for the appropriate time and space to implement and integrate the four components? And how is your program design grounded in the needs and characteristics of the community and of the participants?

In order to plan for your program's future, you must also be aware of the program's past and current track record on meeting goals. It is essential that you have in place from the start an ongoing program evaluation system that measures the progress your program is making toward short- and long-term goals, and that helps you identify and develop new goals and methods for achieving them.

Continuous Program Improvement

There are many program outcomes, such as increasing funding or gaining access to newer technology in the classroom, that you may wish to achieve either in the short- or long-term. These can and should be a part of your program's goals from the start. One of the most important goals of a program concerns the continuing development of your staff, which includes both educators and administrators. The best resource a family literacy program can have is a well-trained staff, who are not only excellent in the classroom but who serve as spokespeople for the program out in the community. As you're formulating your anticipated program outcomes, be sure to consider plans for staff training and technical assistance. Your outcomes may also help you identify areas where staff need specific training, such as work-related learning or parenting education.

Particularly if your program is already operating, you may want to consider outcomes that will help your program run more smoothly or productively. For example, do you want to improve your evaluation system or create a new simplified record-keeping plan? Are there collaborative partnerships you would like to pursue for a specific purpose, or new services you would like to be able to offer, such as free transportation or donated legal services for participants? Is there new technological equipment that you feel your classrooms should have? Are there methods that will bolster your recruitment and retention efforts? Are there funding sources that you would like to make contact with? Are there events you would like to pursue to raise community awareness of the program? Would enrolled families benefit if you integrated work experience into the program? Any of these goals are appropriate to document in your anticipated outcomes.

Launching a family literacy program is a complex procedure, and keeping a program up and running in a consistent, proactive and productive manner is an equally complicated process. Determining goals and identifying anticipated outcomes for the program will help you deliver quality services consistently and will set you on a healthy course of continuous program improvement.

You probably have a very long list now of all the anticipated outcomes you'd like to incorporate into your program! Again, be practical, and if you think you might not be able to achieve a particular outcome this year or next, keep it in a file for future outcomes. Determining your program's anticipated outcomes, and the outcomes expected from each of the four components, like most steps in family literacy, is an ongoing process.

Chapter 5:
Elements of Design—
Putting the Pieces in Place

You now have an impressive list of anticipated outcomes for your family literacy program, and you're just bursting at the seams to open your doors. Great! But there are some very practical elements that need to be in place before you're ready to start helping families attain their goals. We're talking now about the Who, Where and What of a family literacy program.

Logically, you need people to teach your students, a place where you can hold classes, and things to use in the classroom—or staff, site location and equipment. This section will discuss some very basic guidelines to consider when setting up this practical side of your program, remembering that every program and the population it serves is unique. As always, consider the strengths and goals of the families, as well as existing resources in your community, as you decide how best to design your program.

We can't deny that money plays a big part in coordinating all the resources, including people, that you need to construct a strong family literacy program. By involving your collaborative partners in the decision making process, though, you will likely find some creative solutions to many of your challenges.

Staffing

Before you can start interviewing potential staff, you'll have to have some sense of what your program requires in terms of the number of staff, including administrative personnel, and their areas of expertise. It's also helpful to have a plan in place for recruiting qualified staff, starting with ways to locate that staff. What sources are available locally (and possibly nationally) for attracting and supporting staff? Financially, you'll need to not only consider appropriate salaries, but also benefits and professional development opportunities. Ultimately, to determine who your staff needs to be, you will have to consider the goals of your target population. For example, will you be working with preschool or elementary school-aged children? Do you have many adult students who have infants and toddlers? Are your adult students primarily interested in obtaining a GED or becoming employed? Will you have students who speak languages other than English?

The role of Program Coordinator (this might be you!) is essential. Be sure to determine the specific duties of the Program Coordinator. Generally, a Program Coordinator will work directly with all collaborating partners and organize their efforts, in addition to managing program details, supervising the staff and guiding professional development for the staff. This position usually requires a full-time staff member who is organized, thoughtful, articulate, detail-oriented, has keen critical thinking skills, and is comfortable in the role of champion for the program. A Program Coordinator is always looking for new ways to keep a program running smoothly and improve its effectiveness—so he or she must have a thorough understanding of family literacy in order to guide staff development and implement strategies for the program's success. As a Program Coordinator, don't forget to address your professional development and training needs, too!

The makeup of your instructional staff will largely be determined by the structure of the program and the students you hope to reach. Are you planning to work with preschool children, infants and toddlers, or elementary school children, or some combination? Will your program incorporate home visits, and if so, what staff will accommodate those visits? Does your program work primarily with adults transitioning to work, and if so, will the program benefit from a vocational or career instructor in addition to an adult education instructor?

In selecting your instructional staff, bear in mind that being a family literacy teacher is different from being strictly a children's educator or an adult educator (although practitioners will likely specialize in one area or the other.) You will want staff members who enjoy working with the entire family, and engaging in roles that go beyond the typical "instructor." Integrating curriculum across all the components of family literacy is essential to the success of a family literacy program, and it requires teamwork from everyone on the staff. Every member of your teaching staff must have a clear understanding of the components, not as they work separately but as they work together as a whole. Curriculum development requires a team approach, which requires team members who are willing and able to share ideas and work collectively. Keeping communication lines open among all the staff is crucial to ensuring that the services your program provides are relevant and comprehensive.

Also remember that teaching expertise and commitment are directly related to recruitment and retention. For many potential participants in family literacy programs, the first point of contact with the program is the instructional staff. Teachers with enthusiasm, knowledge, professionalism and sensitivity will obviously attract more students than teachers who do not have these characteristics. It's important, too, that everyone on your instructional team is familiar and comfortable with your target population.

You must be aware of your local certification requirements. Most family literacy program sites have—at the barest minimum—an early childhood or elementary school educator, a teaching assistant to the children's educator, and an adult education instructor. Many have additional teaching staff such as a career instructor or parent liason, child care staff, and mentors. Often programs utilize volunteers either from the community or from a collaborating organization. Be sure that everyone on the teaching staff meets your local requirements.

Family literacy teachers will be expected to perform other duties that may not seem like they're directly related to teaching, and it's best to be up front about this in the hiring process. Teachers may have to set up rooms, collect or order materials, recruit families, speak at public functions or with the media, make assessments and keep up records, arrange for classroom speakers and field trips, follow up on absentee students, make home visits, write press releases and create brochures, complete reports to funders, take photos and videos, and work and coordinate with other agencies or employers. This is in addition to teaching! While this list could be intimidating, potential hires will appreciate your honesty. Imagine not expecting these duties and finding out about them on your first day at work!

Sample Task List

Below are listed some of the tasks that family literacy teachers routinely—or perhaps, not so routinely!—are asked to perform.

1. Setting up the rooms
2. Collecting materials for learning centers or areas in both classrooms
3. Ordering materials
4. Arranging to have computers set up
5. Organizing schedules for use of computers and limited supplies
6. Collecting enrichment materials
7. Duplicating materials
8. Establishing policies, procedures, rules and expectations
9. Recruiting students
10. Scheduling and making visits in students' homes
11. Visiting agencies to establish public relations
12. Setting up initial training and inservice for staff
13. Fund-raising

14. Assessing students

15. Record keeping

16. Evaluating the program

17. Finding "state-of-the-art" information to validate and update program

18. Arranging for speakers

19. Preparing for parent conferences

20. Conducting conferences

21. Preparing for and documenting planning time

22. Setting up the daily routine

23. Organizing a community advisory group

24. Designing observation and evaluation forms

25. Cleaning up

26. Establishing communication with school personnel

27. Setting up field trips

28. Accompanying students on field trips

29. Calling students who have been absent

30. Setting goals for sessions in which all staff members are present

31. Completing reports

32. Designing brochures and posters

33. Writing copy for newsletters and press releases

34. Taking pictures, videotaping, recording

35. Arranging for Parent Time meetings outside the school setting

36. Coordinating with other agencies involved with the program

37. Maintaining family portfolios

38. Advocating for family literacy at the local, state and national level

We've said it before, and we'll say it again and again: In a family literacy program, teamwork is essential. Working with both parents and children is a complex scenario, and integrating the four family literacy components means integrating staff approaches. Further, the needs of even just one family are often too great and varied for a single person to address. Effective teamwork makes a program stronger. Effective leadership will help make the team stronger. Looking for team members when you begin hiring your program staff and planning ways to support teamwork from the outset are essential for running a program productively and efficiently.

Sample Interview Questions

1. Tell us how your education and experience prepares you for a position in Family Education, working primarily teaching academic and life skills to adults. There will be times when you will be working with the children also.

2. In Family Education, the adult instructor and the early childhood staff work together as a team. Tell us about a successful experience in your career when you were part of a team. Tell us about a conflict you have had in your team and how you resolved it.

3. Home visits are a regular part of the services offered in Family Education. Tell us what you think the value of home visit instruction could be.

5. Tell us how you would handle the following situation: A parent in the program always seems angry when she is in your classroom. She complains about any suggested activity, and is making very little progress toward her goals. What would you do?

6. Do you have any questions for us about the position?

(adapted from questions developed for the Family Education program by Bev Bing,
Jefferson County Public Schools, Louisville, Kentucky)

To have the same vision for the program, all team members should be involved when you and your collaborative partners are developing or revising your mission statement. Also, the team's role in achieving the program's mission statement should be defined in the statement itself (e.g., "Our program works to deliver quality family literacy services to our community through adult education, preschool (or elementary school) education, parenting classes and regularly scheduled parent-child interaction time").

Not only should all team members share the same vision, it's essential that they understand the program's goals and how the program intends to meet those goals. In fact, whenever possible, everyone on the team should have a hand in developing those goals and measuring progress toward meeting them (this may require specific training in the evaluation methods your program will use). Further, the team must have a clear understanding of the families' strengths, needs and goals. This is true for both administrators and educators.

As with any organization or business, your team needs a straightforward personnel or administrative guide that outlines the program's policies and procedures. This guide will not only include administrative responsibilities but should also address the myriad issues that can arise when working with families who are coping with multiple obstacles. What should your staff do if a student has a substance abuse problem? How does your staff identify learning disabilities and address the needs of students with learning disabilities? What are the appropriate and legal steps to take if your staff suspects child abuse or domestic violence? It's best to have procedures in place from the beginning so that your staff can deal with these issues immediately, capably and safely.

Every member of your program's team will have some responsibility in the area of evaluation—of students, of the staff and of the program. Be sure these responsibilities, as well as other responsibilities and expectations, are clearly spelled out to each team member.

Remember, your family literacy team, in the broadest sense, may be composed of staff, administrators, parents and children, advisory board or steering committee members, collaborative partners, center directors, counselors, social service workers, school principals, volunteers and others. It's important to keep your team well-informed and well-trained. But it's particularly important to pay attention to your instructional team and schedule time for team planning. Your instructional team is the front line in family literacy, and the better they work together, the better they'll work for families.

Site Selection

Site selection is more than randomly picking a place to hold classes. As always, the driving force behind appropriate site selection is your target population. Because family literacy strives to honor parents' educational goals as well as their children's, the program site must be a place that is both practical and comfortable for adults. Remember, too, that home visits may be a necessary approach to reach all of your target population.

Accessibility is key—obviously you will want your program to be located in an area that is easy to get to, either by public transportation or other means (which you may have to arrange). Scheduling availability is also an important consideration. If a site is only available every third Thursday at 9:15 pm, you probably want to look for another location. Determining potential sites will likely be based on your collaborative partners' facility options as well as staffing issues, but above all must be based on your target families and their ability to access the site.

Ideally, a site location will have rooms close to each other that are available simultaneously for adult education classes and children's education classes. This will ease staff planning, classroom coordination, and will aid in integration of program components. If, to take part in PACT Time, parents need only walk down the hall into their child's classroom, some of the trepidation will be relieved and the transition time for the adults and the staff will be lessened. However, co-location of classrooms is not mandatory, and often isn't possible. Sometimes, it may not be appropriate to hold adult education classes at the same time as children's education classes, if, for example, the majority of adults work while their children attend school during the day. If classes are located in separate areas of your site, or even at different sites, or if classes must be held at different times of the day, it will simply require a little extra effort in coordination to ensure that all the components are given sufficient attention.

There are other considerations when selecting your program site. It's very likely that your program will not be the only program utilizing this site, whether it is an elementary school, a vocational college or a community center. There may be turf issues if your program is sharing space or equipment with other programs. Hopefully, the site director, chief administrator or school principal is a member of your collaborative team or advisory board, and will help to garner widespread support for the program. Respecting the responsibilities and turf—both physical and philosophical—of other programs will help you gain outside staff acceptance.

You may be leasing a space, or you may have use of a site location donated as an in-kind contribution from a collaborative partner. Be sure to check local requirements for early childhood classrooms if that is your target clientele when you're making these arrangements. Also, it's helpful to define in your contract with the site facility exactly which areas your program can access and at what times. For example, if you wish to hold classes in a computer lab or in the library, what is the scheduling procedure? What are your program's responsibilities for using these areas—should certified staff or security personnel be in attendance?

It's also important to find a classroom or learning area that dignifies the adult student and is conducive to group learning. For example, child-size chairs, cramped space, or individual study carrels do not help in building the confidence and self-esteem in adult students that will allow them to be active participants in their own education. Look for ways to create a comfortable and welcoming learning environment for adults, rich with educational materials and other resources.

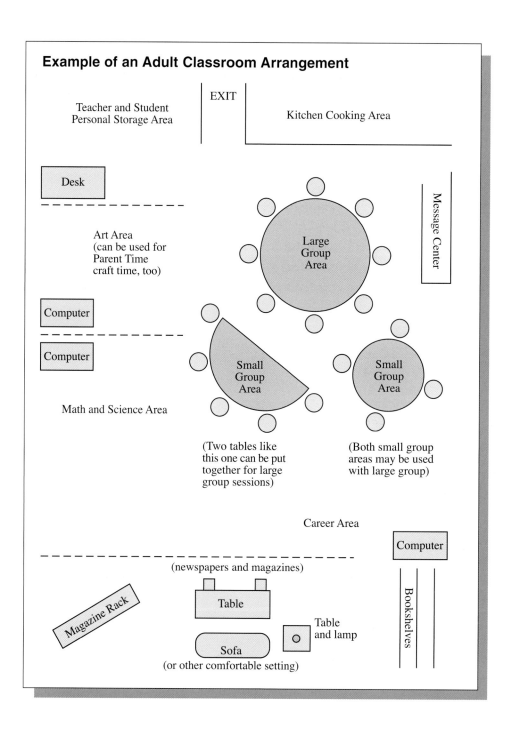

Example of an Adult Classroom Arrangement

EXIT

Teacher and Student
Personal Storage Area

Kitchen Cooking Area

Desk

Message Center

Art Area
(can be used for
Parent Time
craft time, too)

Large
Group
Area

Computer

Computer

Small
Group
Area

Small
Group
Area

Math and Science Area

(Two tables like
this one can be put
together for large
group sessions)

(Both small group
areas may be used
with large group)

Career Area

Computer

(newspapers and magazines)

Magazine Rack

Table

Table
and lamp

Bookshelves

Sofa

(or other comfortable setting)

The key word to keep in mind when selecting a program site is "stability." Some quality family literacy programs have really struggled when their site location arrangements have fallen through. As simple as site selection would seem, having a stable site location is a very practical and necessary part of a center-based family literacy program.

Materials and Equipment

You have educators and administrative staff, you have a place to hold classes, but your classrooms are bare! Well, that's probably not quite the case, but there will be materials and equipment that you want and need to have available. For a family literacy program, you especially want to select materials that will foster literacy in both adults and children, reflect the cultures and diversity of your students, and be relevant to your students' life experiences and goals.

The equipment and materials you use are largely up to your creativity and the creativity of all the staff. Some sample materials that you may need for a preschool classroom are:

- A variety of books that can include picture books, nursery rhyme books, poetry, work-related children's literature (change the selection periodically)

- Magazines and newspapers for children and adults, including discarded magazines that can be cut to create new pictures

- Computers, software and printers

- Tape recorder and accessories

- Stuffed animals and/or puppets, rubber animals, dolls and dollhouses

- Puzzles, geoboards and pegboards

- Sand and water table

- Magnets, scales, magnifying glasses and timers

- Paint supplies, construction paper, markers and other writing utensils
- Musical instruments
- Play dough or clay
- Chalkboards and color chalk
- A variety of building blocks
- Model vehicles, maps
- Model home furniture such as a stove or a washing machine
- Dress-up area with clothing that reflects the local area, citizen and worker roles, and culture(s)
- Role play items such as cash registers and telephones

Be sure also that you have ample storage area for works in progress!

If your family literacy program works with elementary school-aged children, you may not have as much input as to the materials that are available in the children's classroom; however, there will likely be a variety of appropriate materials for fostering literacy development. Hopefully you will be able to use the same or a similar elementary school classroom for PACT Time. Look at the existing materials in the classroom from the adult learner's perspective—how can the classroom be used to encourage interactive literacy activities between parents and children?

For home visits, there will be some equipment that you may want to have on hand, such as books or educational toys. While sometimes you may wish to bring toys or other materials into families' homes, particularly if parents can't afford toys for their children, it may be a more effective strategy to help families identify items in their own homes that can be used for learning. By doing this, you encourage families to work together in creating a learning environment in their own home.

Some household items that may be used in learning activities include:

- Plastic bowls with lids or plastic cups (for matching sizes and colors, nesting and stacking)

- Mirrors (for teaching children body parts, comparing part to whole)

- Clothing (for dress-up, counting, matching color, size and pattern)

- Magazines and newspapers (can be used in numerous activities that include identification and as springboards for discussion)

- Empty boxes (for matching, grouping, sizing, stacking)

- Silverware (for matching, fine and gross motor skills)

- Foods (to identify color, texture, temperature, nutrition)

And don't forget your adult learners! Spend just as much time and attention arranging resources and gathering equipment that will attend to their learning needs. You'll find that adults are more motivated to learn when instruction relates to their individual goals. Since goals vary, teachers and programs need to be flexible. This flexibility should be reflected in the variety of materials available in the adult classroom. Below are some materials you might have available in the adult classroom:

- Paper, pencils, rulers, tape measures, calculators

- Adult education textbooks, reference books, maps and globes

- Newspapers and magazines, high-interest books

- Colored paper, scissors, string, glue, tape

- VCR, tape recorder, television

- Brochures and literature on community and job resources

- Comfortable furniture, and areas designed for individual and group learning

- Computers and printers

Be sure to select computer software programs carefully—try them out yourself. Software can be expensive and you don't want software that is unusable or inappropriate for your students and their skill levels. If appropriate, have software available that has practical or work-related applications, such as word processing, spreadsheets, and graphics programs, as well as educational programs that work to develop literacy and numeracy skills. Access to the Internet is a tool that more and more educational programs are finding essential. It opens up a world of (free!) resources. (If you're unfamiliar with on-line literacy resources, here are three good ones to try: The Literacy List – http://www.alri.org/literacylist.html, Gateway to Educational Materials – http://thegateway.org, and Dave's ESL Café – http://www.eslcafe.com.)

Again, the resources you need will be determined by your staff and their creativity, and should reflect the students' goals and interests. While some of the materials you need will probably have to be purchased, you may be able to have many items donated by your collaborative partners or other concerned agencies and organizations in your community. You may also want to publish a "wish list" through school newsletters, church bulletins or business bulletin boards.

Supporting Services

The focus of the practical side of designing a family literacy program is always on making it as easy as possible for the maximum number of families to take part in the program. Two services that frequently and directly affect accessibility for families are transportation and child care.

Many families do not have or are not aware of reliable transportation available to them, and this may be one major barrier preventing them from attending a family literacy program. It may be necessary to develop a transportation plan that will allow more families to access your program.

Your students may be able to use public transportation. Some programs, working with their local public transportation authority, are able to furnish discounted passes to their students to use public transportation. Other programs offer students compensation for their mileage if they have to drive to reach the program.

When public transportation is not available, some family literacy programs are able to make arrangements through schools or churches to use buses and vans. Other programs are able to purchase their own van for transporting students. In either case, you will have to check local regulations and your insurance to be sure that the transportation your program is providing complies with all safety requirements. Be sure also that whoever is responsible for driving a program vehicle has the appropriate type of driver's license.

Often parents who attend family literacy programs with their preschool or elementary school-aged children also have younger children who require care. In order for these families to attend a program, parents have to make child care arrangements for their younger children, either through an outside agency or through the family literacy program itself. Many adults in family literacy programs can't afford professional child care. Others who are able to find appropriate child care off-site may experience scheduling conflicts as they try to juggle home life, work life and family literacy classes. To begin addressing your program's child care options, you may want to meet with your collaborative partners to see what solutions you, as a group, can provide.

Some family literacy programs offer infant and toddler services. These services provide literacy and learning experiences for both the infant or toddler and the parent, as well as physical care for the infant/toddler. If your program provides these services, you must adhere to state guidelines, insurance guidelines, and the requirements of your funding sources. Even when not required by law, child care licensing regulations provide basic standards for health and safety that your program will want to follow. Before pursuing this option, you may also wish to explore the Head Start Program Performance Standards, many of which offer guidelines for specific, physical child care requirements for Head Start programs.

Another option for addressing the needs of your adult students with very small children is to make arrangements with a professional child care agency to offer child care on-site or nearby. You may be able to arrange these services through one of your collaborative partners. Again it must be stressed that any child care services that your program offers, either directly or indirectly, must comply with local health and insurance regulations, for the safety and well-being of the children in the program.

A third possibility is that a family literacy program may want to focus more on home visiting rather than being primarily a center-based program. For families facing obstacles such as lack of transportation, child care or conflicting work schedules, home visits may be an effective way to meet their educational needs. For some families, especially in rural areas, home visits may be the only way they can participate in family literacy programs.

In addition to addressing participants' accessibility issues, home visits offer valuable opportunities that can enhance a family literacy program's overall effectiveness in meeting families' needs. Home visits allow instructors to interact with families in familiar settings, and they help to support the concepts of lifelong learning and creating a learning environment in the home. Keep in mind, as you are considering what place home visits have in your program design, that home visiting services—like center-based services—are structured, well-planned times to interact with families in pursuit of their educational and non-educational goals. Home visits require teamwork, integration and evaluation, just as much as family literacy components that occur in centers or schools.

Many families enrolled in family literacy programs are eligible for free or reduced-cost meals—adult students as well as children—and this too can make a family literacy program more accessible and attractive to families who have few resources and difficult schedules. Explore this possibility with the school or community-based organization, or your collaborative partners.

Chapter 6:
Strategies for
Success

One of the biggest challenges to running a family literacy program or any service organization is maintaining momentum—momentum that will keep your program solid and moving forward. This momentum doesn't necessarily happen naturally, much as we may wish it did. Like all functions in a carefully designed family literacy program, strategies to maintain and continually improve your program must be well thought out, even before you begin enrolling students.

Planning for the future is critical to ensuring the lasting success of your program. Specifically, there are five areas that need to be addressed in your strategic design: staff development, management, evaluation, recruitment and retention, and raising public awareness. By working out the details in these areas now, you'll be building a strong foundation for your program's future.

Of course, the instruction your students receive will play a large part in their motivation and their success, and therefore the continuing success of the program. In family literacy, as in most educational approaches, keeping instruction timely and relevant is an important strategy for maintaining interest and encouraging progress. There are a number of good resources to aid you in developing instructional strategies, including NCFL's *The Family Literacy Answer Book*, Jobs for the Future's *Work-Related Learning Guide for Family Literacy and Adult Education Organizations*, and the *Equipped for the Future Content Standards* from the National Institute for Literacy. Staff development is also central to the continuous improvement of instruction.

Staff Development

Ongoing staff development is vital to your program. Education is a constantly changing discipline, as new research informs our practices and as students' goals change to reflect the society in which they live. Staff development is a way to keep your program connected to the world outside the classroom while staying connected to the students in the classroom.

Staff development is a perpetual process—it doesn't (or shouldn't) end when the seminar is over or when you've finished reading an article. It involves personal development, as in studying current educational research and keeping up with events in your community, as well as professional development that improves specific skills in teaching, facilitating, leadership and teamwork.

There are several kinds of staff development—training opportunities, on-site technical assistance, conferences, seminars, workshops, teleconferences, Web-based instruction or satellite broadcasts—and you should pursue them all! There likely will be development opportunities in your area of expertise. For example, you may be particularly interested in a seminar on ways to utilize the latest brain research to improve reading instruction, or a workshop that offers approaches to incorporating work-related literacy activities for adults transitioning from welfare to work.

Your entire staff, including administrators, should attend general training that provides a comprehensive picture of family literacy overall. This sort of training will not only introduce strategies for effective teaching but also strategies for improving the other crucial layers of family literacy, like component integration, recruitment and retention, teamwork and evaluation.

Speaking of evaluation, you will want to use your evaluation system to identify areas where staff skills can improve in order to continue meeting the needs of your students. For example, if a majority of your adult students have as one of their primary goals to earn their GED, and if those students are not obtaining their GEDs within an appropriate timeframe, then perhaps your staff needs additional training to expand their techniques in addressing basic skills for adults. Evaluation will guide you toward the kinds of staff development that will keep the program on target to help students meet their goals.

You should also find opportunities—or create opportunities—to orient your collaborative partners to family literacy, and this too is an ongoing process. Everyone with even a peripheral association to your program, e.g., social workers or the local librarian, needs training to become familiar with what family literacy is and how it works. This will help make them more valuable contributors, which makes your program stronger and more effective.

The best way to guarantee that your staff will have ample opportunities to increase their skills is to plan staff development just as you would any other facet of your program. That is, what are the outcomes the program wants to achieve and what tools can your staff use in order to achieve those outcomes? One of the roles of the Program Coordinator is to be aware of what the staff's strengths and needs are—both individually and as a team—and to provide strategies for improvement. This formula boils down to two essential ingredients: time and money.

To elicit enthusiasm for staff development, you must take into account that it takes time, often time in addition to an already overflowing workload. It may require traveling, which means more time, and it most definitely will require follow-up activity, which takes even more time. However, quality staff development is time well spent! Scheduling staff development in advance will allow you to work it into your staff's regular routine, so that it is not perceived as an "additional" duty. For instance, many programs use Fridays as a flexible day for planning, home visits or professional development. If this isn't possible, or even if it is, provide stipends for extra hours and time spent traveling. And be sure to offer opportunities for your staff to choose their own areas of development—maybe a staff member has a particular interest in technology, or another staff member wants to expand the program by working with incarcerated parents. Your staff can also help prioritize development strategies that will keep classrooms relevant and instruction practices current. Honoring your staff's time will encourage them to see staff development as a benefit, not a chore.

Work staff development into your program's budget or grant proposal in the early stages—and be prepared to defend that line item! Money is always tight, and some of your funders or board members may see development as expendable. Just as you do in designing other elements of your program, have clear goals in mind—how staff development will improve and expand your program to better help your students reach their goals—and communicate your anticipated outcomes to any skeptics.

Here, too, evaluation can come to your rescue. Part of your evaluation system should address staff development as it applies to your program's progress, to help you strategize and support your development plans. How will you measure progress? How will you assess staff skills in your program? What outcomes of your students can help you identify areas of weakness or strength in your program? Below are some specific examples of staff development issues that evaluation may help to clarify or solve:

1. You've noted that standardized assessment scores are not rising: is the test administered correctly? Does it align with what is being taught?

2. Retention is very low. When you study those students who leave the program before completing their goals, you find that a majority of them performed in the lowest literacy levels at the time they entered the program. This may warrant staff training in recognizing and addressing students with learning disabilities, or teaching very basic reading.

3. An outside observer notes that the adult classroom is reminiscent of the "old school" of teaching—adults sitting in rows, teacher standing at the front of the classroom delivering a lecture. Staff may need training in active learning approaches or "Teacher as Facilitator" training.

There are numerous sources for staff development, provided locally as well as nationally, by private organizations and government associations. There are professional workshops and seminars available throughout the country on a variety of topics that relate to family literacy, from reading acquisition research to project-based literacy to respecting cultural diversity to policy affecting families in need. Conferences can not only provide a wealth of information, but also serve to rejuvenate, another important purpose of staff development. When conferences are attended by a team, they help to build camaraderie. On-site technical assistance will allow professional "outside" observers to assess your program's day-to-day activities and offer specific, hands-on advice.

Note: The Program Coordinator may not have control over what type or how many staff development opportunities individual team members may have, either because they report to a different agency or because of union or organizational rules. Still, it's advisable to pursue as many staff development opportunities as appropriate, although you may have to get permission and "buy-in" from other organizations or supervisors.

Program Management

Once a program is up and running, the only way it will stay up and running is if someone, or some agency, is responsible for ensuring that the program is maintained. Much that is included throughout this guide applies to overall program management. Clear roles for each agency and collaborating partner must be established and communication lines must be kept open among all active collaborators. Many of the program management duties will fall to the Program Coordinator, who helps to tie all the pieces of a family literacy program together.

Be sure that there is a management plan that not only defines and assigns responsibilities for the day-to-day operation of the program but also sets program goals and monitors progress toward those goals. Never assume that everyone involved in a family literacy program knows what everyone else is doing—as we've said, family literacy is a complex process that draws from many resources, all of whom may have "their own way of doing things." Someone, usually the Program Coordinator, has to be in charge of enforcing policies and standards, to keep the program (and everyone involved) moving toward common goals.

Part of your management plan will include not just what evaluation methods you will use, but *how* you will use them—to improve teaching approaches in the classroom, to identify areas for staff development, to guide specific and/or broad program adaptations, and to keep participants and funders informed of progress.

Evaluation

We struggled with the placement of evaluation in this guide. Too often, it's left until the end—of the book, of the program—when in fact it really must be addressed at "ground zero." We have placed evaluation here because it is a strategy—maybe *the* strategy—for keeping your program current, productive, accountable, and continuously improving. However, we cannot emphasize enough that planning for evaluation is an integral part of the entire program development process.

Evaluation can map out a course for success as you and your students reach toward the attainment of specific goals. An effective evaluation plan will inform your students on their progress while helping you to assist them more effectively. It will help your students determine future goals as they learn to assess their own strengths. It will inform other interested stakeholders in your program—the school board, collaborative partners, funders, the media, and the general public, for example—about your students and your program. In short, there is a wide range of questions frequently asked about family literacy that a well-designed evaluation can answer:

- Where and how is your project situated in the organization? Where is it located physically and on what schedule does it operate? Who are your collaborative partners and what services does each provide?

- Who are the administrators? Who are the staff members? What are their roles? What are their special capabilities? What are the significant staff or staffing limitations?

- Who are the clients? What are their characteristics? What criteria are used to identify and select clients?

- What services will your program provide? Are there any services required by clients that your program cannot provide?

- What assumptions have you made about the changes you expect to see in your clients? What causes those changes to occur, or allows them to occur? How long do those changes usually take? How are short-term gains and lasting benefits related? Are positive changes actually occurring in students and families? What evidence do you have that these changes are the result of your program?

- Did you adopt a model program? If so, what are its features? Are you implementing the model as it was designed? If not, what changes are you making? Why are you making those changes? If you adopted a model program and changed it, what evidence do you have that the changes did not affect the expected outcomes? Are there any unexpected, unexplained, or indirect effects of your program?

- What are your reasons for believing the program is adequate in terms of intensity and duration to cause the client changes you expect?

- How is this program different from other programs that serve similar clients with similar needs and interests? What assumptions have you made about why your program is better than others for serving these clients?

- What are the resources allocated to the project? What resources actually are required? How have these resources been allocated?

- What is the curriculum and instructional approach for each component of your program? What materials are used in the program?

- What are key decision areas for the program? How are key decisions made? Who makes those decisions?

As stated earlier, evaluation should begin on "Day One" of program development, and the first evaluation activities most likely will exemplify *process evaluation*. Process evaluation examines program structures, staff, materials, curricula and activities, and is especially useful in assessing overall program implementation. In other words, are the processes of the program effectively bringing about progress towards achieving your program goals?

Much of your evaluation plan will undoubtedly focus on participants and their achievements, particularly within the four components of family literacy. *Outcome evaluation* examines the immediate or direct effects of the program on the participants and is usually the type of evaluation in which "outsiders" such as funders will be most interested. Student outcome evaluation may assess gains in knowledge or skills or improvements in attitudes or behaviors. Program outcomes could include the number of families served, average daily attendance, and retention of families.

Impact evaluation looks beyond process and outcomes to determine either long-term or indirect program effects. For example, family literacy programs designed to help welfare recipients obtain employment may conduct follow-up student surveys to investigate issues of job retention and promotion.

Before you determine your evaluation plan, explore existing data such as school records and prior assessments. Not only will this save you time, it can also help to identify the gaps in data collection that bolster arguments for support of a more comprehensive evaluation system. It is not uncommon for student intake to be done in one place—such as a social services office—and basic skills assessment in another. Become aware of all the places where data is being gathered on the families you're enrolling and try to share that information as much as possible so that repetitive forms and assessments are minimized.

Also, before you commit to a particular evaluation method, be sure to check local and state regulations. There may be limitations as to what sort of evaluation you're allowed to perform and issues such as confidentiality or parental consent for children that need to be considered.

There are some very basic steps to take when establishing your evaluation system:

1. Lay the groundwork in initial staff training by discussing the importance and purpose of evaluation with all staff.

2. Involve staff in planning for evaluation, determining goals and objectives, and selecting measurement instruments and other data collection procedures.

3. Ensure that every staff member understands his or her role in the evaluation plan.

4. Continually train staff members to collect and record data regularly and consistently, and keep staff informed of revisions to the evaluation plan.

In planning your evaluation system, first determine what question or questions you need to answer (the list at the beginning of this section is a good starting point). Keep in mind the issue of "need" versus "want." There may be a long list of things you and your staff want to know about your program, but it's best to focus—especially in the beginning—on what you need to know. You may find that collecting the "need to know" information is all that's feasible at first; as the program matures and staff gains experience, some of the "nice to know" elements can be added to the evaluation plan.

Next, consider what kind of data you need to collect in order to answer these questions and what methods you can use to collect this data. These may be in the form of tests, student and community demographic data, questionnaires, interviews, recorded observations, student artifacts, teacher logs, and program data such as budgets and staff résumés. The collected data will then need to be analyzed—this may need to be performed by an outside evaluation specialist—to determine the answers to your evaluation questions.

Working with a contracted outside evaluator can be tricky, but can also be rewarding if planned carefully. First, develop a list from the evaluation plan pinpointing exactly which evaluation tasks will be performed in-house and which activities will require the services of a contractor. Once this list is developed, the role of the contractor will likely become clarified. Usually, the outside evaluator will be hired to execute a well-defined list of activities or will serve as a general technical assistant for all evaluation activities, which could even include initial program design. One of the biggest stumbling blocks for programs as they pursue a relationship with an outside evaluator is not clearly defining everyone's responsibilities from the beginning. The written contract should clearly outline the activities and deliverables expected of the contractor over a given period of time.

Once all the data has been appropriately analyzed, you must determine how your findings will be reported. Your reporting methods should reflect the needs of your intended audience. If the information is of particular interest to staff, you may want to have an in-house presentation and discussion of the findings. If your evaluation is intended to meet requirements of funders or the school board, you may need to present the findings in a formal report. An evaluation report can even take the form of a press release if your findings are of interest to the media and general public. Of course, staff will determine how to best keep the families informed of their individual progress toward their goals, one of the most valuable uses of evaluation. You will need to report your findings in a variety of ways to address a multitude of audiences.

What follows are some other important, but by no means exhaustive, considerations for implementing an effective evaluation system. Evaluation is a complex but crucial part of family literacy, and it requires commitment from all staff. In order for evaluation to be an effective tool for both accountability and continual improvement, the plan must be well designed and thoroughly executed. Only valid and reliable data are useful.

Both students and teachers may provide information in a way that they think will be most positive for the program. While their intentions are good, a less-than-accurate response only jeopardizes the usefulness of the evaluation as a strategic tool. Similarly, as you report findings from an evaluation, it's important to be objective—reporting negative findings should not be considered as criticism of the program but rather a necessary insight to program improvement. It is also crucial that data collection be complete in order to obtain accurate information, as incomplete data is essentially invalid data.

Evaluation planning and data collection take time, and this time must be accounted for in your program design. Keep all staff actively involved throughout and informed of preliminary findings so that they can use this information both in the classroom and with other stakeholders. Staff can also help to clarify findings that are puzzling since they have direct knowledge of the conditions surrounding the findings. Finally, it may be useful to arrange evaluation training for staff.

A number of useful tools are available to inform the evaluation process. For in-depth information on participant assessments, you may want to refer to NCFL's publication *Outcomes and Measures*. Even Start's *Guide to Quality*, prepared by RMC Research Corporation, includes a program self-assessment tool broken into categories that match the Even Start quality considerations in the guide, such as "Collaboration," "Home Visiting," and "Staff Development."

Recruitment and Retention

If you build it, they will come. That, unfortunately, is not always the case with families targeted for family literacy—families whose lives are complicated and hectic, who may be facing a number of difficult issues, who may have experienced failure in educational settings in the past. The key to recruitment and retention is communication—getting the word out, getting the word out again, and keeping the word out.

The "word" is a very clear message about your program's capabilities. That message should be shaped to address parents' needs, interests and goals, as parents are their families' leaders and will ultimately make the decision whether to enroll or not. The word should also be honest, straightforward and culturally appropriate.

It's time once again to pull out your trusty community assessment to use as a tool to direct your recruitment efforts. The better you know and understand your community and the families you wish to serve, the better you'll be able to communicate how your program works to meet their needs. If your community has a large population of speakers of languages other than English, get the word out in their languages. If your community has many families with very young children, get the word out that your program has child care options. If your community is adjusting to welfare reform, get the word out about how your program offers opportunities that qualify as work experience.

Be sure that your description of the program is realistic. A sure way to disappoint, and subsequently lose students, is to promise gains that you cannot deliver. Recruitment must be conducted with *retention* as the goal—remember that quality family literacy programs are "of sufficient duration, to make sustainable changes." Getting students into your classrooms is only the very first step—an important step, to be sure, but retaining students in the program is the only way to "make sustainable changes."

Recruitment takes effort and it takes time—especially initial recruitment. Be patient, and be thorough. Contact families face to face whenever possible, and enlist the help of other community agencies, including your collaborative partners, as well as all of your staff.

Referrals from other agencies or from a central intake and assessment center may account for the bulk of your participants. Keep in mind that the staff at those centers need to be aware of what your program offers and which potential (and eligible) students will benefit from family literacy. As this staff can change, informing these agencies, either through written literature or, better, in person, needs to be done on an ongoing basis.

Reciprocally, you need to be aware of whether and how your program meets other agencies' referral criteria. This is particularly true for TANF agencies. If this is your target audience, be sure that your program design meets their criteria.

Also, tell community leaders, or "gatekeepers," all about your program so that they can help spread the word. They are often in direct contact with many of the families you think your program can serve.

And be creative! Generating excitement about family literacy can be a lot of fun! What follows are just a few examples of recruitment activities.

- Alert the media! Send press releases and public service announcements to radio and television stations, newspapers, school and church newsletters. Go on the air to promote your program.

- Post flyers in high traffic areas like laundromats, apartment complexes, churches, gas stations and stores.

- Identify qualified families through social service agencies (but be sure to ask about confidentiality issues first).

- Go door-to-door. Take a Polaroid camera with you, and, with permission, take two photos of each family you meet. Write your program's name and phone number on one photo and leave it with the family. Write the family's name on the other photo and take it with you, so that you can greet them by name when they come to enroll.

- Set up information tables at fairs, discount stores, school festivals and other community events. Be sure to have printed materials available to take, and something to entice customers—a video playing on a monitor, or something free to give away.

- Have an open house (but not until your program is ready!) Be sure that it's culturally relevant and packed with fun activities that get people moving and talking to one another.

- Have a "beginning of the year" ceremony to make new students feel welcome and to encourage retention by emphasizing a commitment to the program.

- Empower current participants as recruiters—word of mouth may be your most powerful recruitment tool!

There are a few basic guidelines to stick to when designing printed materials, which are a very valuable and fairly inexpensive way to advertise. Make sure they are visually appealing, with eye-grabbing headlines and pictures. The information should be brief but complete. Include your program's phone number (maybe as a tear-away tag)—and then make sure that there is a knowledgeable and friendly person available to answer that phone! The person who answers the enrollment/information phone is often the very first contact a family has with the program. This person needs to know as much about the program as possible to answer any questions. Keep your flyers and other printed materials interesting, but never with false hype. Write in the language or languages of your community.

Now you have loads of students enrolled in your program. Congratulations! How are you going to keep them coming back? We know that the families who enter family literacy programs are often struggling with immense pressures that make a regular schedule difficult to stick to. But we also know that if they don't commit to the program, and return throughout the year, they won't thoroughly benefit from it. How do we gain their commitment to the program?

Well, first, we ask for it up front. Students and staff can make an oral or written commitment to each other and to program participation (this is true for students enrolled in home-based programs as well as center-based programs). This agreement may include not only a commitment to attend the program, but also might outline policies such as respecting other participants in the program, confidentiality from staff and participants, and expectations and responsibilities of both staff and students. Perhaps you can have an "agreement signing" celebration at the beginning of the year to emphasize the importance of commitment to the program.

City/County Family Literacy Program

What Can Family Literacy Offer You?

✓ Adult Education and English as a Second Language Classes

✓ Education for Your Children (age 8 and under)

✓ Training for You in Helping Your Child Learn

✓ Learning Activities for You and Your Children

What Else Can This Program Offer You?

✓ Free Child Care (6 months–3 years, during program hours)

✓ Free Family Health Screening

✓ Free Home Visiting Sessions

When and Where Does the Program Meet?

Classes begin September 12

Monday through Thursday, 9:00 am until Noon

Local Elementary School or Community Center

325 West Main Street

How to Enroll

Call the phone number below between 9:00 am and 5:00 pm,
Monday through Friday. All calls are confidential.

City/County Family Literacy Program: 555-5555 | City/County Family Literacy Program: 555-5555 | City/County Family Literacy Program: 555-5555 | City/County Family Literacy Program: 555-5555 | City/County Family Literacy Program: 555-5555 | City/County Family Literacy Program: 555-5555 | City/County Family Literacy Program: 555-5555 | City/County Family Literacy Program: 555-5555 | City/County Family Literacy Program: 555-5555 | City/County Family Literacy Program: 555-5555 | City/County Family Literacy Program: 555-5555 | City/County Family Literacy Program: 555-5555 | City/County Family Literacy Program: 555-5555 | City/County Family Literacy Program: 555-5555

The quality of your program will definitely have a lot to do with your retention rates—no one is going to return to classes that aren't relevant or interesting, or where they feel unwelcome or patronized. Staff must be culturally aware and sensitive to the many issues in families' lives. Personal attention should be paid to each student individually, and students should never question the confidentiality within the program or between the program and other agencies. Family literacy programs should be safe and comfortable for all participants.

Home visits should be part of your program's routine not only to monitor educational behaviors in the home but also to demonstrate a willingness to make the extra effort. Home visits are a way to stay connected to the circumstances in which your families live, and also may give you the opportunity to meet and talk with other family members who are not enrolled in your program, but whose support can help your students stay enrolled.

Often there are people of strong influence in adult students' lives—a significant other or spouse, a parent, sibling or close friend. It takes courage to enroll in a family literacy program, and soliciting the support of the "others" in their lives can be crucial to keeping adults enrolled in a program. Invite family members and friends to a program celebration to enlist their support of the student. Take pictures (with permission!) of the whole family and arrange a place in your classroom for photographs and personal/family artifacts to be displayed. Help others understand that their support is needed and appreciated by you as well as the student.

While you will be guiding your students in goal setting, remember that ultimately they will determine which goals they want and need to pursue. Using your evaluation system, keep your students motivated by keeping them informed of their progress towards these goals. Offer small incentives to achieve particular goals—from getting to choose the Circle Time activity at the conclusion of PACT Time, to homemade certificates of achievement. Some programs mimic worksites, offering program "dollars" for achievements, redeemable at a program "store" stocked with donations, books or other incentives. Plan for an end-of-year celebration to recognize all of the individual and family accomplishments—invite all the members of each family to attend, and serve refreshments afterwards.

Whenever possible, connect the classroom experience to real-life experience, and help parents understand the importance of all four family literacy components. If you don't know how your students feel about the program, ask them! Interview students to learn ways that you can make the program more useful to them.

Plan for ways to keep students coming back—every day. If someone is absent for a day or two, contact them. Invite graduates back to speak to current students or to continue in some aspect of the program. Recruitment and retention are both ongoing processes. The time to develop retention strategies is not when you start losing students—it's before you enroll even your first student. You will also find that retention is your best recruitment tool. The more satisfied your students are with your family literacy program, the more likely they are to recommend it to friends, family members and neighbors. Remember, word of mouth is probably the strongest recruitment tool you can have.

Raising Public Awareness

There is a very simple reason for raising public awareness in your community. The more people know about family literacy, the more they are likely to support your efforts. This support can manifest itself in monetary or service-based contributions. Public awareness can also help give your program good visibility within your community, which will aid recruitment efforts. And it never hurts to let your elected officials know about the power of family literacy!

The most obvious way to raise awareness is through the media—newspapers, radio and television. But it's not as easy as it sounds. Press releases are the best way to communicate with the media; however, the information you are divulging must be considered newsworthy or it won't be printed or broadcast.

How do you know if an event or accomplishment is newsworthy? Ask yourself:

1. Is the information of general interest to readers *not* connected with family literacy programs?

2. Is it about something that affects the lives of the public, or specifically people in your community, in some way?

3. Is the substance of your release something unusual or out of the ordinary?

If you can answer yes to any of these questions, your press release probably contains "legitimate" news.

Remember that the editors to whom you send your press releases receive hundreds—maybe thousands—of releases every day. You know you're doing important work and that the events you've planned are exciting and essential. Now you have to get that across in a (very short) press release to a potential reader who doesn't know anything about family literacy. Keep press releases brief (one page is best) and interesting, and avoid adding hyperbole or opinions. The press release is intended as an informational tool only.

If you're publicizing an event, mail your press release about four business days before the event (you don't want them to forget about it, but you also need to give them enough time to assign a reporter to the story, or run the press release "as is" a day or two before the event.) Send press releases to a specific contact at each newspaper and station, and always follow up the mailing of your press release with a phone call to see if your contact has any questions.

Planning and executing an event in your community is a great way to attract media, politicians, celebrities, potential students and the general public. You may want to tie an event to a special day, like National Family Literacy Day® on November 1, or you may want to schedule a site visit for local businesspeople or community officials to give them a personal look at how family literacy operates.

Sample Press Release

(Print on Your Program's Letterhead)

FOR IMMEDIATE RELEASE

Contact: Mary Jones
(502) 555-5555

LOCAL FAMILY LITERACY PROGRAM TO CELEBRATE
NATIONAL FAMILY LITERACY DAY®

(Louisville, Kentucky, October 15, 2000)… The City/County Family Literacy Program is celebrating National Family Literacy Day® (NFLD) on Wednesday, November 1. In observance of NFLD there will be a "Read-a-thon" at the Free Public Library on November 1, 9:00 am until noon. Parents are invited to bring their children to this free event to take part in fun literacy activities, including storytelling, a puppet show, and arts and crafts based on favorite children's books. Every family will receive a free coloring book to take home.

National Family Literacy Day® is celebrated around the country with special activities and events that showcase family literacy programs and the important relationship between parents and their children. Family literacy is a unique approach to education that draws on the strengths of families and brings parents and children together in the classroom to improve their skills and support each other's learning.

The City/County Family Literacy Program offers families adult education, including GED preparation and English as a Second Language; preschool children's education for ages three and four; a time for parents to meet and discuss their children's literacy development; and Parent and Child Together Time, when parents and children play and learn together in the classroom. The Program is free for eligible families with children ages three and four. For information about enrolling in the City/County Family Literacy Program, call 555-5555.

National Family Literacy Day[1] is sponsored by Toyota. Over the last nine years, Toyota has given nearly $16 million to establish family literacy programs across the country. The Free Public Library and The Local Superstore are providing support for the City/County Family Literacy Program celebration at the Free Public Library.

###

Because you want to give the best possible impression of your program, it's important to organize your event carefully. First, sit down and make a list of all the people in your community who might be able to contribute their time and talent to your event. Compile a list of contact names and separate them into categories: public officials, business leaders, community leaders, educational leaders, parenting organizations, and so on. Once you have this list, determine who would be appropriate to invite to what sort of event. For example, a politician might embrace the opportunity to read a children's book out loud at a gathering at the local library whereas the Dean of the Education Department at the local college might benefit more from visiting a PACT Time session.

Also, when planning a public awareness event, consider the outcomes you hope to accomplish, then tailor your event to attain those outcomes. If your overall goal is to increase recruitment, orchestrating a site visit for the Mayor is probably not the most productive use of your energies.

Remember: You are the authority on family literacy in your community, and the media and other interested parties will be looking to you for answers. Make sure you have them—both in your head and in printed form. Here are a few questions to ask yourself before you send out press releases or invitations to events—the basics to cover about family literacy in your community:

1. How many families do you serve?

2. What hours and days do you operate?

3. Describe the population and community the program serves.

4. What services do you offer?

5. Why is it important to offer comprehensive services? What kinds of challenges do the families face?

6. How do you measure the success of the program?

7. How do you work with the entire family?

8. How is family literacy different from adult education or children's education?

9. What is your staff's expertise in serving families?

10. What are the specific outcomes anticipated for families in your program?

11. Have you measured the success of the program? Tell a story about individual families and parents overcoming educational barriers.

12. How many years has your program been in operation?

13. Why does your program need significant funding increases?

14. Describe how you feel about the impact of the program on the families you serve.

15. How can both the public and private sectors support family literacy?

16. How many families in your community are in need but are not receiving family literacy services?

Probably the most important part in planning your public relations efforts is to involve your students and staff—after all, it's really their program that you're promoting, and they will probably have some excellent ideas about how you can reach your intended audience. Without a doubt, students make the most powerful speakers for family literacy. Their stories are the ones that will motivate others to get involved.

Raising public awareness can help your program attract the attention it deserves from a wide variety of potential supporters. For more suggestions on raising public awareness, visit the "Advocacy" section on NCFL's Web site: www.famlit.org.

Chapter 7:
Journey to
Success

Family literacy is a remarkably powerful approach to working with economically and educationally disadvantaged adults and children. The outcomes for families enrolled in family literacy programs can be tremendously positive and far-reaching, helping parents gain economic stability and starting children on a path of lifelong learning.

Most of us who practice family literacy do so because we want to make a difference—in our community and in the nation. We want to help families break free of the barriers caused by a lack of education, and we know that family literacy is the approach that can reach those families. We've watched as parents and children learn together, and we've shared their joy.

We also know that family literacy is a lot of work—for the rewards to be great, the challenges must also be great. Family literacy involves loads of paperwork, legwork, and plenty of brain work. But we also know that there is a growing field of experienced and talented family literacy practitioners throughout the country, an ever-increasing body of research and best practices. There are also more and more opportunities to bring new partners into the fold.

Most importantly, we know that family literacy does make a difference. We hear the stories of parents who have gotten off welfare and stayed off welfare, whose children have stayed in school and who are achieving academic success. We hear stories like Sara's, who didn't speak English when she first enrolled in a family literacy program, but went on to earn a Bachelor's Degree in bilingual education and whose children are honor students in school. We hear stories like Dorothy's, who went from being a high-school drop-out with two children by the age of 19 to being an employed computer programmer with one daughter excelling in school and another daughter ready to graduate from high school herself. There are hundreds—thousands of other encouraging stories from the halls of family literacy.

But there are still thousands of families who, for many different reasons, are not getting the help they need, through family literacy or any other service. The families who slip through the cracks—these are the families we must work harder to reach.

This guide has provided the starting points—the building blocks—for initiating and maintaining a quality, comprehensive family literacy program. While it certainly does not include all the information you will need to ensure the permanent success of a family literacy program in your community, we hope that it answers many of your questions about designing an effective family literacy program and planning for future success.

The appendices that follow contain an overview of National Center for Family Literacy initiatives and concrete examples of innovative program adaptations that may provide you with further inspiration and guidance in designing your program.

While we offer you all the encouragement we can muster, we thought it best to let someone else share their story of success with you. The following is excerpted from testimony given by former family literacy student Raynice Brumfield, who participated in the Toyota Families for Learning program in Washington, DC. Her continuing success as of this printing is indicative of the enduring power of family literacy.

"Thank you Senator Jefford and members of the Senate Committee, for inviting me to share my story with you. By virtue of the fact that I can sit before you to take part in this occasion, proves that without a program like the Toyota Family Learning Tree, I would still be just stuck in the house, taking care of my two small children, faced with a future that didn't look bright.

"I am Raynice Brumfield. I am a 25-year-old single parent with four children; James 10, Delonte 8, Kiara 5, and Tyrone, age 4. I was born in Washington, D.C., and attended the public schools there. When I was 15 years old I became pregnant with my first child. Between the ages of 15 and 17, I worked at various jobs. I soon found that I could not make enough money to afford food, clothing, baby supplies and living expenses. At age 17, I became pregnant with my second child. By 19, I enrolled in one of the District of Columbia's public vocational schools. I dropped out of that school because the staff was not sensitive to the needs of young mothers, and I did not feel safe in that environment. I started to receive Public Assistance when I was 19, and soon became pregnant with Kiara, and the next year, Tyrone.

"The opportunity to further my education, while being close to my children, seemed like a dream come true. On September 30th, 1996, my children and I started school. The adult education teacher (Mrs. Grace Blackwood), and the parenting instructor (Mrs. Irene Ball), greeted me warmly. I was quiet, scared, and very unsure of myself.

"When I entered the program my reading and math levels were at a second grade level. My teachers, and the program's coordinator, Mrs. Peggy Minnis, made the other parents and me feel like we could accomplish anything. They made sure that we maintained a positive self-esteem. We were encouraged to set goals, and they helped us work to meet each goal. The work was hard, but soon it became a daily routine for my children and me to sit at the kitchen table, learning together. As my reading skills improved, I began to enjoy reading stories to my children at home, and going into their classroom to practice and share my new skills with any child who wanted to crawl up in my lap, to hear me read. The harder I worked, the easier it became to help my older children with their homework. I began taking part in the activities at their school. My children's home library grew from 2 or 3 books to over 40. Reading stories or telling stories to my children has helped in their language development and provided me with practice in reading.

"The parenting course helped me understand child development. Understanding the stages that my children were going through helped me to be patient, understand, and able to predict their behavior. I learned that there are whole new worlds that my family and I can explore for free. We visit these new worlds every weekend inside the public library. I tell my children that even though we don't have a lot of money, we can still visit far away places and people. Most importantly, we enjoy these adventures as a family. All of my children have their own library cards. I've become a responsible citizen who has a voter registration card and I vote.

"As a result of being in the Toyota Family Literacy Program, new worlds have opened up for me and my family. Worlds that were once just part of my daydreams are now a reality. I am proud to tell you that I now read on a 10th grade level, and my math skills have increased to a 9th grade level. I received an award from my children's school, which honored me as being "Most Active Parent in Schoolwide Activities." I have volunteered more than 200 hours in my children's school. My children's report cards and teacher comments are no longer negative but positive. I was invited to speak at last year's 27th Annual congressional Black Caucus Legislative Conference in Washington, DC, by New Jersey's Representative Donald M. Payne. I shared how Toyota, through the National Center for Family Literacy and the Head Start Program, is helping to improve literacy in the African American community by focusing on young children and their parents. That speech was placed on the E-mail system of every congressman and representative in Congress…

"In January, the Head Start Program invited me to be a guest speaker at their staff development activities. Again, I told how family literacy programs make futures bright. I just took the GED examination on the 16th.

"My adult education teacher encouraged me to apply for an intensive training program through the YWCA's Non-Traditional Jobs for Women Program last school year. I was accepted into the program, and have completed the training, which prepared me to be trained as a carpenter, plumber, mason, or electrical worker.

"Upon notification of having passed the GED, I have been promised priority consideration for a non-traditional job at George Washington University (in the District of Columbia) through a partnership that has been set up between our program and the university. I will have the opportunity to work for no less than $12.00 per hour, have paid leave and benefits for my entire family. I will gain experience, meet new people, and most importantly, have the opportunity to continue my education free of charge. Upon advancement in my job, my children will be able to attend George Washington University and get their college education for free.

"The partnerships between Head Start, the National Center for Family Literacy and the Toyota Corporation have made my future look bright. By nurturing the promise of providing a quality education to my children and me, they have given me empowerment through literacy."

Raynice Brumfield
Testimony before the Senate Committee
on Labor and Human Resources
April 28, 1998

Nurturing. Promise. Quality. Empowerment. These eloquent words from Raynice and the stories of families like hers give hope to the future, a future shaped by educational opportunities for multiple generations. Family literacy provides a pathway to success for families. That path may occasionally wind and bend, there may be fences to hurdle or crevasses to jump. But in the end, the journey is well worth it, and the pathway of family literacy leads to the road of lifelong learning for parents and children—together.

Appendix A:
NCFL Projects and
Program Adaptations

One of the strengths of family literacy is its adaptability, making it an especially effective approach to meeting the needs of diverse populations. Whether in urban or rural settings, highly industrial or agricultural environments, in primarily English-speaking communities or communities where members speak a number of different languages, family literacy can help improve educational and non-educational opportunities for both adults and children from a variety of cultures. The power of family literacy is that it recognizes that all families have strengths, and strategically builds on those individual strengths.

Key to the success of family literacy programs is acknowledging and respecting family differences so that program development and curriculum evolve from focusing on families' strengths rather than on perceived weaknesses. Subsequently, family literacy programs must be flexible in order to best meet the goals that students set for themselves as well as to achieve program outcomes that are acceptable to other stakeholders.

For more than a decade, NCFL has taken part in and pioneered several exciting family literacy projects that have helped shape the national movement, perpetually broadening the scope and reach of family literacy.

Toyota Families For Learning Program

Over the years, Toyota has given nearly $16 million in support of family literacy through the National Center for Family Literacy. The first project to unite Toyota and NCFL, which would set the pace for family literacy program development across the country, was the Toyota Families for Learning program.

The Toyota Motor Corporation provided a grant to NCFL in 1991 to establish the Toyota Families for Learning program in five cities: Atlanta, GA; Pittsburgh, PA; Richmond, VA; Rochester, NY; and Tucson, AZ. Based on the successes in these initial cities, Toyota awarded another grant in 1992 to expand the program to five more cities (Seattle, WA; Dallas, TX; St. Louis, MO; Ft. Lauderdale, FL; and New Orleans, LA) and funded still five more cities in 1993 (Chicago, IL; Denver, CO; Nashville, TN; Little Rock, AK; and Los Angeles, CA.) In the years since these initial investments, Toyota has helped NCFL bring Toyota Families for Learning to Lexington, KY; Washington, DC; Long Beach, CA; Ontario, CA; and Cincinnati, OH—bringing the total number of cities in the project to 20.

Essential to the design of this program was an innovative approach to funding that provided start-up funds to support a three year incubation period at each location. This period of development included intensive training and technical assistance for program staff. Having a secure base from which to build allowed sites the time to nurture collaborations locally that could sustain operations following those first three years. To date, Toyota Families for Learning programs are still operating in each of the original communities, and those programs have impacted countless other programs in the communities and across the nation. The practice of incubating programs while they generate self-supporting systems has been standard practice in every model program initiated by NCFL since 1991.

Toyota Families in Schools Program

In 1998, the Toyota Motor Corporation provided a grant to NCFL to develop a family literacy model for elementary schools. This project, the Toyota Families in Schools program, is designed to bring about fundamental changes in the interaction between schools and the parents of students from low-income families. With an emphasis on instruction for parents as well as children, the goal of Toyota Families in Schools is to root family literacy firmly in the nation's major school reform efforts. In November, 1998, NCFL and Toyota announced the selection of partners for the development year for the project: Rochester City School District, Metropolitan Nashville City Schools, St. Louis Public Schools, Sunnyside School District in Tucson, and Seattle Public Schools.

Building on the parental involvement commitments between schools and parents, Toyota Families in Schools challenges educators and administrators to view parents in a different light. It also challenges parents to learn ways to support their children's education by improving their own education. Following the first successful year of program implementation, five additional school districts joined the project: Jefferson County Public Schools (Louisville, KY), Houston Independent School District, Los Angeles Unified School District, Kanawha County School System (Charleston, WV), and New Orleans Public Schools. In 2000, five new school districts were selected to join the Toyota Families in Schools program: Aurora Public Schools (Aurora, CA), Richmond City Public Schools (Richmond, VA), Fremont Unified School District (Fremont, CA), Broward County Public Schools (Ft. Lauderdale, FL), and Evansville-Vanderburgh School Corporation (Evansville, IN). The addition of these five school districts brings the total number of Toyota Families in Schools program sites to 45.

Family And Child Education (FACE) Program

In 1990-1991, the Bureau of Indian Affairs Office of Indian Education Programs (BIA OIEP) brought together three national organizations in an unprecedented collaborative effort to improve the educational opportunities for American Indians. The Family And

Child Education (FACE) program draws from the expertise of the Parents as Teachers National Center, the High/Scope Educational Research Foundation and NCFL to provide education, resources and support for American Indian families with children from birth to grade three. Training and on-site technical assistance have been at the heart of the FACE program since its inception and remain a cornerstone of this longstanding initiative.

The collaboration among these three organizations plus the BIA OIEP has not only provided a strong professional development structure for staff of the FACE program, it has also served as a model for teambuilding and networking that any family literacy program can learn from. The FACE program has also informed the way that NCFL and other family literacy practitioners work with culturally diverse populations. As of 2000, there were 22 FACE sites at BIA schools in nine states which serve students from many different Indian tribes, including Navajo, Lakota Sioux, Kickapoo, Potawatomie, Choctaw, Puyallup, Pima and Ojibwe. The FACE program focuses on infusing local culture and Native language to ensure that services are always relevant to the individual communities where the sites are located.

Knight Family Education

The John S. and James L. Knight Foundation joined the family literacy movement in 1994 with a grant to open programs in Ft. Wayne, Indiana and Akron, Ohio. Like the Toyota Families for Learning project, these programs were funded for three years, with assistance and training to help them become self-supporting at the conclusion of those three years. Through the project, NCFL explored issues facing families in smaller cities, and found them to be identical to big city issues.

Family Independence Initiative

In 1997, NCFL embarked on a new three-year journey to help lead families into the next century through the implementation and evaluation of family literacy programs that are adjusting to welfare reform. With a $2.25 million grant from the John S. and James L.

Knight Foundation, NCFL established the Family Independence Initiative, which works to address the needs of families affected by the 1996 Personal Responsibility and Work Opportunity Reconciliation Act (PRWORA).

Through a planning grant from the Knight Foundation, NCFL investigated the impact of welfare reform on family literacy programs and built an action plan for placing family literacy at the center of reform. In the Initiative's first year, welfare reform adaptations were studied in five development sites in McCormick, SC; Eau Claire, WI; Canton, OH; Rochester, NY; and Ft. Wayne, IN. Based on the experiences of these development sites, NCFL issued a request for proposals from programs that wanted to test a work-focused model of family literacy. In the summer of 1998, NCFL announced five new Family Independence Initiative pilot sites: Akron, OH; Boulder, CO; Charlotte, NC; Long Beach, CA; and Philadelphia, PA. NCFL also continued its partnership with Canton, which would continue to serve in a mentoring capacity.

The Family Independence Initiative is a comprehensive approach to helping impoverished families adjust to new federal and state policies regulating public assistance, bringing a focus on work into the classroom for children as well as adults to aid families transitioning from welfare to work. Practices developed through the Family Independence Initiative have informed NCFL's work in all other areas. Key to the Initiative's success has been the wide dissemination of best practices through trainings, policy briefings and publications.

UPS Family Education Program

The UPS Family Education program, begun in 1995 with funding from The United Parcel Service Foundation, was designed to study family literacy's effectiveness under varied circumstances, from a large metropolitan area to an isolated rural community. The program funded nine family literacy programs in Atlanta, Louisville, and the rural McCreary County in Kentucky. All of the programs completed the final year of the initial grant cycle, and have continued to offer family literacy through local funding sources.

Careers for Families

In 1998, The UPS Foundation funded the Careers for Families program. This project works to tie family literacy programs in Louisville to community business partners in order to develop an employment-oriented family literacy program that can be replicated in other cities. Key to Careers for Families' success is establishing these partnerships with area businesses in order to inform programs on how best to equip parents to become stable employees, particularly parents who are moving from welfare to work or who have little or no work experience.

The project aims to develop employment connections that match participants' work goals with available jobs, and explores issues of combining work and learning for those struggling to become independent. The first participants in this program began work in January, 1999. Through a variety of research strategies, NCFL is gleaning information that will guide other programs in connecting families to job placement. As of this writing, plans are being developed to implement Careers for Families in two new cities—Atlanta and Philadelphia—in 2001.

For more information about the Careers for Families program, please see the case history in the following appendix.

Parent-Child Interaction Project

In 1994, NCFL teamed with the Louisville Science Center and the Jefferson County Public Schools Family Education Program in Kentucky to initiate the Parent-Child Interaction Project. The project was designed to evaluate the effectiveness of programs involving learning among parents and children in science centers, with an emphasis on mathematics and science. This project served as the groundwork for an expanded Parent-Child Interaction Project in 1997, when the National Science Foundation (NSF) awarded a planning grant to initiate projects in Atlanta, Ft. Lauderdale, Nashville, Pittsburgh, Rochester, St. Louis, and again in Louisville.

The South Carolina Head Start Family "Independence" Literacy Collaboration Project

From 1996 to 1999, NCFL worked with South Carolina to develop and explore the role of family literacy in welfare reform, specifically with Head Start programs. South Carolina state and local agencies developed a collaboration to promote, maintain and improve ten rural family literacy projects. The state team, in consultation with NCFL, identified objectives for the programs which included implementing a four-component program connected with a Head Start program, having a strong focus on welfare-to-work preparation for adults, and supporting adult participants as they are placed in jobs. A local team participates in joint training for program implementation, secures the commitment of local resources, plans and coordinates services, and monitors progress.

Head Start Family Literacy Project

The Head Start Family Literacy Project is a five-year cooperative agreement that will assist Head Start programs to enhance and expand the delivery of family literacy services as defined in federal legislation. Begun in 1999, the project will build on Head Start's existing training and technical assistance network to deliver research-based family literacy training. The management of the project relies on a collaboration between NCFL, the Head Start Bureau, the Head Start Quality Improvement Centers (HSQICs) and RMC Research Corporation.

As parents acquire new educational, social, employability and life skills, they are able to enhance the literacy skills of their children. Family literacy becomes one pathway to economic stability. The Head Start Family Literacy Project is designed to support the continued efforts of Head Start through training, technical assistance, the development of a Promising Practices Network, and creating new resource materials.

Appendix B:
Case Studies in Work-Focused Family Literacy

The following case studies provide examples of how family literacy programs are meeting the needs of the welfare-to-work population. Since the passing of the Personal Responsibility and Work Opportunity Reconciliation Act (PRWORA), many family literacy programs have had to adapt to meet new requirements of welfare reform, which affects a large part of family literacy's overall target population.

Family literacy has been shown to be an effective strategy in helping families—adults and their children—transition from welfare to work and gain economic stability. Adaptations have included curriculum shifts in all of the components, as well as program design shifts that address parents' working schedules and the need for facilitating broader collaborations, especially with welfare agencies, community employers and employment agencies. What has been clear from the start to family literacy programs and practitioners is that getting a job and getting an education are not isolated issues. When addressed together, parents and families have a greater likelihood of attaining economic independence.

Case Study 1: Long Beach, California

One way for family literacy programs to incorporate career planning, pre-employment skills and job placement services is to collaborate with the local provider of those services.

In June of 1998, the Family Literacy Program (FLP) run by California's Long Beach Unified School District (initially a Toyota Families for Learning program site) joined forces with the City of Long Beach's Welfare-to-Work program to create LiteracyWorks. The purpose of the LiteracyWorks partnership is to maintain a comprehensive, integrated, four component family literacy program while engaging Welfare-to-Work and Temporary Assistance for Needy Families (TANF) participants in pre- and post-employment work activities in order to prepare them for self-sufficiency.

Parents in LiteracyWorks attend adult basic education, PACT Time and parent education at an elementary school or the Long Beach School for Adults, which also offers occupational training. Their young children participate in an Even Start or Head Start preschool based on the High/Scope model. For parents to be able to find and retain work, FLP staff knew parents needed to explore career paths, gain work skills and connect with employers.

Through this partnership the FLP participants are connected to the Career Transition Center (CTC), a "one-stop shop" for employment services. (Both the CTC and the Welfare-to-Work program are part of the Private Industry Council.) This model "one-stop" has a resource center with employer and employment information such as the California Cooperative Occupational Information System (CCOIS). The CCOIS analyzes labor market information for 50 occupations that match employer needs with job seekers' skills. The CTC also provides computers, fax machines, copy machines, telephone banks—everything needed to complete a job search. In addition, the CTC offers vocational and career assessment, career counseling, on-the-job training, work experience and computer training. The Welfare-to-Work program also provides child care and transportation, follow-up support, and workshops on such topics as résumé writing, job application skills, interviewing skills, and how to keep a job.

For the families, the link between the CTC and the family literacy program is facilitated through a Literacy Liaison. Funded through NCFL's Family Independence Initiative (made possible by the John S. and James L. Knight Foundation), the Literacy Liaison functions as a case manager, guidance counselor and recruitment/referral source for all eligible participants. To ensure that these disparate services appear seamless to families, a collaborative administrative team consisting of the FLP Director, Welfare-to-Work Coordinator, Head Start Assistant Director, and the Program Evaluator meet monthly to coordinate overall administrative activities and oversee effective program implementation.

LiteracyWorks also forged ties with the Department of Public Social Services (DPSS), the state agency serving TANF clients. This extremely important relationship was bolstered by the placement of a DPSS service worker on-site at the Career Transition Center two days a week, serving as a direct contact for client certifications and client issues.

In this way, the Long Beach family literacy program has built on existing community resources to provide families with career guidance, connections to employers and specific work opportunities, and social services. This has allowed the family literacy instructors to focus on integrating a work focus into the curriculum. Importantly, while combining all of these resources, Long Beach has been able to centralize services, which makes it easier for families to access the services they need.

Case Study 2: Canton, Ohio

The goal of Canton City Schools' Even Start program is to break the intergenerational cycle of poverty and undereducation through an integrated approach focusing on:

1. Improving basic literacy, numeracy, and employability skills of parents;

2. Promoting children's developmental growth through children's education; and

3. Empowering parents to promote their child(ren)'s cognitive, social/emotional, language, and physical development.

Canton City Schools is the ninth largest school district in the state of Ohio. In the school year of 1998-99, Canton's Even Start served 58 families with the following statistics:

- 97% female

- 65% white, 32% African American, 3% Asian

- 90% on welfare (TANF)

- 0% employed full-time, 3% employed part-time

- 48% entered at literacy level I (0-5.9), 52% at level II (6.0-8.9), 0% at level III (9.0-12.9)

In the same school year, average adult attendance was 328 hours.

Canton's Even Start program is built on existing school district and community resources. The school district's community education department provides career assessment and academic/workforce development education. Title I funds provide enhancement of services for the children and parent-child learning activities from the Parent Resource Center. The Department of Human Services assists with recruitment of families and funds child care for children under age three and wrap-around care. The local newspaper donates free papers for learning activities. Community business partners help motivate students, fund incentives and awards, and provide shadowing opportunities for parents to explore careers. Students from Malone College acquire field experience hours while assisting in Even Start classrooms. Mercy Medical Center provides health screenings and information and is the host site for Canton's job shadowing experience. The Ohio State Extension Service provides nutrition and homemaking lessons.

Families in Canton's Even Start come to school together at their neighborhood elementary school. The adults attend 30 hours a week in their own classroom within the elementary school building. Most families in this urban program walk, but parents are permitted to ride school buses or are given passes for the city bus service when necessary. Public preschool for three- and four-year-olds is also located within the elementary schools. Neighborhood child care centers transport children under age three to and from the elementary schools and provide developmentally appropriate programming for these children.

In response to welfare reform, Canton's Even Start, one of five development sites in the first year of the Family Independence Initiative and a mentoring site in subsequent years, focuses on work-based learning. In Ohio, welfare recipients must participate in work and educational activities for 30 hours weekly, twenty hours in work activities while the remaining 10 hours may be fulfilled through additional work or adult education. Canton's program combines work and education into a 30 hour work-based learning site at the elementary school. Parents participate in real work experiences in and around the elementary school community. Development of communication skills, interpersonal skills, decision making skills, and lifelong learning skills is emphasized during these work experiences. Academic skills are taught in context as they are needed for the students to fulfill their roles as parent, worker and citizen (the roles outlined by Equipped for the Future). As parents acquire new skills in one role they learn to apply them in other roles. For example, parents improve communication skills within their family and transfer these new skills to the workplace. Because the primary work sites are their children's schools, parenting education and PACT Time are easily integrated into work experiences.

Realizing that most of Canton's Even Start parents will need to be employed before they can earn their GEDs, Canton is helping each student develop an Individual Career Plan which identifies a realistic initial job, future career goals, and a plan for reaching those goals. The process begins with career assessment and continues with work-based learning activities. Career development activities including mentoring, job shadowing, career exploration, and development of a Career Passport assist the student in preparing to attain and maintain initial employment. The Career Passport, which documents the skills a student has demonstrated, helps certify to employers the student's qualifications. "Reunions," a weekly post-employment support group funded by the Family Independence Initiative, assists graduates in maintaining employment and balancing the responsibilities of family and work. The evening includes a free nutritious dinner and parent-child activities. While children then take part in literacy activities, parents meet together to discuss the day-to-day challenges they encounter and to support each other in problem solving.

Canton's commitment to family literacy doesn't end in the classroom. By drawing on existing local resources and collaborations, and by approaching curriculum development creatively, the Canton Even Start program has successfully integrated family literacy and state welfare reform requirements. Families receive services that not only support and enhance their pre-employment efforts, but also services that meet their post-employment needs.

Case Study 3: Louisville, Kentucky

Careers for Families, a work-focused initiative developed by NCFL with funding from The United Parcel Service (UPS) Foundation, is creating a model employment-oriented family literacy program in Louisville, Kentucky. This model engages the business community in welfare reform efforts and family literacy while helping parents gain the skills they need to get and retain jobs. A major focus of Careers for Families is a seemingly simple and practical one: to match participants' work goals with available jobs in the community.

Collaboration was, at the outset, a key element in the development of the initiative, and was fostered in the earliest stages of planning. Relationships were quickly established with the Workforce Development Council, the Jefferson County Department of Human Services, the Department of Social Insurance, the Entry Level Workers Consortium, and the Jefferson County Public Schools system. A thorough community assessment was conducted in order to clearly communicate to businesses and other agencies that Careers for Families would not be duplicating existing services and that it would reach a population that other programs could not or would not reach.

It was determined early on that Jefferson County Public Schools (JCPS) had an employment-oriented family literacy education program already in place which could provide a springboard for this welfare-to-work strategy. During negotiations with JCPS administrators and their Board of Directors to formalize the relationship between JCPS and NCFL Careers for Families, JCPS Family Education staff began discussing program design details.

Several questions were posed. What enhancements were needed in the curriculum, both for adult education and early childhood education, to meet the expanding needs and goals of families? How would new Careers for Families students matriculate into existing programs, or how could Careers for Families be offered to returning students? How would career planning and mentoring be structured? What staff development was necessary, and how would this be addressed? Also during this time, the director of the Family Education program agreed to attend meetings with potential employment partners to discuss the integration of work with the initiative's educational component.

When the NCFL Careers for Families-JCPS agreement was approved, a career instructor/mentor was hired. This instructor began interviewing TANF recipients for interest in enrollment, and also worked with the program coordinator to forge employment partnerships and to develop the career planning component of the initiative.

Several valuable collaborative partnerships were nurtured throughout the planning stages and initial year of program implementation. By the end of the first year, five diverse employment partnerships (JCPS, UPS Air District, Jewish Hospital, Papa John's International and Target Stores) had been established that offered a variety of career opportunities. Many complicated issues were raised as these relationships grew, including options for career development, assigning on-site mentors for Careers for Families student/employees, class locations, day care opportunities, and company benefits.

In the wake of welfare reform, new collaborations are essential for meeting the needs of a population in transition. In Careers for Families, the director of the Department of Human Services forged the connection between Careers for Families and the Entry Level Workers Consortium (a group of about 75 employers who face common problems in hiring entry-level workers), which brought about partnerships with three large local employers. In addition, the JCPS Family Education program coordinator meets with case managers at the TANF agency on an ongoing basis to develop a system for referrals for TANF recipients. This connection has allowed Careers for Families to develop work experience and employment opportunities that meet TANF requirements while allowing families to attend family literacy programs to reach their academic goals.

The partnership with Jefferson County Public Schools has been crucial to the development of Careers for Families, because, like all quality family literacy programs, the emphasis is on education. In the case of this initiative, education—specifically family literacy—has been seen from the start as the pathway to gainful employment. The communication between JCPS administration, JCPS Family Education staff, business partners, the Department of Human Services, and the NCFL Careers for Families project manager has been essential to meeting all the needs—educational and non-educational—of the families.

Many crucial steps have been identified in the first year of Careers for Families program implementation, some of which particularly pertain to employment-focused programs, others that are applicable to all family literacy programs. Below are just a few:

- Examine the community's welfare reform efforts to date. What programs already exist? What agencies operate those programs? How are they funded? What programs have proved most effective and why? What services seem ineffective?

- Start with who and what is known. In the planning stages, brainstorm with colleagues and other professional associates. This can lead to other contacts in the community. Contacts make more contacts, and word-of-mouth is extremely valuable in establishing new partnerships.

- Contact business organizations such as the local Chamber of Commerce or Workforce Investment Board (formerly Private Industry Council) for literature about your community's labor needs, present and future—particularly information that will identify organizations who regularly employ entry-level workers. Attend networking meetings or offer to host a meeting to present a Careers for Families-type program and survey the needs and interests of local businesses.

- At the start, seek out businesses that already recruit TANF recipients. Find out if businesses in the community think of TANF recipients when considering their labor pools. If not, why not? Ask them to explain their hesitations or concerns as specifically as possible.

- Listen carefully to what businesses have to say. Learn from their experiences, and identify common themes among the businesses in the community. Know what areas businesses are looking for in new-hires: what qualities and specific skills do employees have to possess? Offer ways to support the changing needs of the businesses.

- Create a menu of partnerships in a variety of industries. Seek to offer parents a selection of job opportunities that represent varying skill levels and be clear about specific requirements for each job (e.g., background investigations, drug tests, credit checks, etc.) Conduct worksite investigation activities and invite business speakers to present during Parent Time.

- Develop an ongoing media strategy to educate and inform the community about the exciting opportunities created by these partnerships. Apprise the local media (newspapers, business journals, television) and spread the word about the program through community bulletins and school newsletters. Attend community networking opportunities, and ask to be on the agenda to give a five-minute overview of the initiative.

The Careers for Families program is truly a community initiative which uses the platform of family literacy to engage new partners and expand the network of opportunities available to families. Parents receive instruction and experiences that make employment a tangible goal, based on the practical needs of real-life potential employers. As this model is expanded into new cities, the ways that employment can be thoroughly integrated with family literacy will no doubt expand as well.

Appendix C:
Questions to Guide Your
Family Literacy Action Plan

What follows are "nuts and bolts" questions to guide you, program staff and collaborating partners in forming an action plan for a family literacy program. Use them to discuss specific aspects of implementing family literacy services and to help in creating an overall program plan for delivery of those services.

Community Needs

1. What are the educational and non-educational goals of families in your community?

2. What programs are currently addressing those goals?

3. Are there gaps in service delivery or any duplication of services to families?

4. How would a family literacy program fit into your community network?

5. What model best suits the needs of the community and the goals of the families?

6. What resources will be necessary to support this program?

Collaboration

1. Who are the members of your collaboration?

2. Are there other agencies that should be added to your collaboration? How will you approach them?

3. How will you increase the awareness of family literacy issues and this program's goals among your collaborative partners?

4. What steps can be taken to assure that your collaboration is an active partnership?

5. How will partners determine what they will give to and what they will receive from the program?

6. What turf issues exist? How should boundaries be erased or honored?

7. What can be done now to lay the groundwork for continued funding? For future expansion?

Other?

Administration

1. Who are the key administrators (school, agency, business, etc.) that must "buy into" the program to ensure its success? How will they receive the necessary background on family literacy and the program?

2. How does the program fit in the larger picture of serving families in your city?

3. Has the Program Coordinator been determined or will that position be a newly hired one? (This should be determined as soon as possible.)

Site Selection

1. What criteria will you use for selecting sites for the program? Do the key people at each facility have ownership?

2. What must be accomplished to prepare the physical environment for the program?

3. As you think of the four components (adult education, children's education, Parent Time, Parent and Child Together (PACT) Time), are there any aspects that should be addressed in site preparation?

4. How will you assure the acceptance and support of other staff members at the facility?

Other?

Staff Selection

1. What are the steps necessary in hiring staff for this program?

2. How will the process differ from other hiring procedures? Are there multiple funding sources involved? What is the equity of schedules and pay?

3. How will you determine whether potential staff members are team players?

4. How will the Program Coordinator be involved in hiring staff?

Other?

Staff Development

1. How will your staff prepare to maximize the time spent in implementation training?

2. How will you respond to ongoing staff development needs?

Other?

Program Planning

1. How will team planning be encouraged? Does the budget accommodate time for weekly team planning for staff and home visits to families?

2. How will you accommodate the interaction among all family literacy sites in your city?

3. How will you determine the daily and weekly schedule of students and staff?

Other?

Program Evaluation

1. What are the specific goals of your program? What outcomes do you anticipate for individuals and for families?

2. How will you measure each goal?

3. Who will be responsible for data collection and reporting to funders?

4. How will results be used with students, collaborators and others?

5. Do you have additional areas of interest in research that you would like to pursue?

Other?

Transportation/Child Care/Meals

1. What do your students require in areas of transportation, child care and meals? How will the program respond to these needs? Funding?

2. Which partners can work with the sponsoring agency in these areas?

Other?

Recruitment and Retention

1. What are the recruitment strategies you plan to employ now? What will be the ongoing strategies?

2. How will you inform "gatekeepers?"

3. How will teachers be involved in recruitment?

Other?

Equipment and Materials

1. What existing equipment and materials will be used?

2. What materials need to be ordered? Though what agency?

3. What timeframe will ensure that delivery of materials and equipment will take place prior to program opening?

Other?

Index